Great American Writers

TWENTIETH CENTURY

EDITOR

R. BAIRD SHUMAN
University of Illinois

James Agee • Julia Alvarez

Sherwood Anderson • Maya Angelou

Margaret Atwood • James Baldwin • Saul Bellow

MARSHALL CAVENDISH
NEW YORK • TORONTO • LONDON • SYDNEY

Marshall Cavendish
99 White Plains Road
Tarrytown, New York 10591-9001

Website: www.marshallcavendish.com

Salem Press

Editor:	R. Baird Shuman
Managing Editor:	R. Kent Rasmussen
Manuscript Editors:	Heather Stratton
	Lauren M. Mitchell
Assistant Editor:	Andrea Miller
Research Supervisor:	Jeffry Jensen
Acquisitions Editor:	Mark Rehn

Marshall Cavendish

Project Editor:	Marian Armstrong
Editorial Director:	Paul Bernabeo

Designer: Patrice Sheridan

Photo Research: Candlepants
Carousel Research
Linda Sykes Picture Research
Anne Burns Images

Indexing: AEIOU

Library of Congress Cataloging-in-Publication Data

Great American writers: twentieth century / R. Baird Shuman, editor.
    v. cm.
    Includes bibliographical references and indexes.
    Contents: v. 1. Agee-Bellow--v. 2. Benét-Cather--v. 3. Cormier-Dylan--v. 4. Eliot-Frost--v. 5. Gaines-Hinton--v. 6. Hughes-Lewis--v. 7. London-McNickle--v. 8. Miller-O'Connor--v. 9. O'Neill-Rich--v. 10. Salinger-Stein--v. 11. Steinbeck-Walker--v. 12. Welty-Zindel--v. 13. Index.
    ISBN 0-7614-7240-1 (set)—ISBN 0-7614-7241-X (v. 1)
    1. American literature--20th century--Bio-bibliography--Dictionaries. 2. Authors, American--20th century--Biography--Dictionaries. 3. American literature--20th century--Dictionaries. I. Shuman, R. Baird (Robert Baird), 1929-

PS221.G74 2002
810.9'005'03
[B]   2001028461

Printed in Malaysia; bound in the United States

07 06 05 04 03 02   6 5 4 3 2 1

Introduction

This encyclopedia is for students of fiction, poetry, drama, nonfiction, and song lyrics who wish to learn more about the most influential and significant twentieth-century writers of Canada and the United States. Some of the writers covered here were born in the nineteenth century, but all of them did their most important writing and publishing in the twentieth century.

Turn-of-the-century authors, such as Theodore Dreiser, Jack London, Frank Norris, and Upton Sinclair, represent the spirit and vigor of the new age that dawned in both society and literature around the turn of the century. They all published in the twentieth century. They broke from the nineteenth century's genteel tradition in literature, forging ahead into a new realism and beyond it to the literary naturalism that characterizes the most important writing of the first half of the twentieth century.

Works by the authors included in these volumes frequently appear in school and college anthologies or have had a profound influence upon some of the most notable authors of the twentieth century. Among the authors in this encyclopedia who influenced later authors, Gertrude Stein looms large. Her impact upon language and writing style directly affected the writing of many authors of the so-called "lost generation" who gathered in Paris after World War I, among them Ernest Hemingway and F. Scott Fitzgerald.

T. S. Eliot, Robert Frost, and Langston Hughes had a comparable impact upon poets who followed them, notably Wallace Stevens, E. E. Cummings, Nikki Giovanni, and Maya Angelou. Eugene O'Neill, the playwright who single-handedly spawned serious American drama after 1920, later touched directly the writing of such dramatists as Tennessee Williams, Arthur Miller, and Lorraine Hansberry.

The Early Twentieth Century. As the nineteenth century drew to a close, North American society was changing rapidly, moving from agrarian, farm-based economies to industrial economies that drew millions of people to crowded cities that were often ill-equipped to meet the newcomers' needs for housing and services. Europeans, knowing that burgeoning industries needed workers, rushed to the United States and Canada seeking work.

American literature reflected much of this social and economic upheaval. For example, Frank Norris chronicled the death grip in which all-powerful American railroads and commercial cartels held farmers and workers. Upton Sinclair focused on the plight of uneducated immigrant workers, writing with such realism about conditions in the U.S. meatpacking industry that reading *The Jungle* (1906) caused many Americans to retch. This novel led to the passage of the federal Pure Food and Drug Act of 1906 shortly after U.S. president Theodore Roosevelt read the book.

Theodore Dreiser shocked readers by choosing as the protagonist of his novel *Sister Carrie* (1900) a woman of easy virtue who, rather than receiving retribution for her moral laxity, achieved success and lived a life of luxury. The genteel tradition that had characterized the preceding generation of writers communicated little that people in rapidly expanding urban settings valued.

A new morality was creeping into the writing of a fresh generation of writers. These authors adopted a heightened realism that culminated inevitably in literary naturalism, which views human behavior in terms of economic, genetic, and social determinism. The evolutionary theories of English naturalist Charles Darwin and the psychological writings of Austrian psychiatrist Sigmund Freud and

Swiss psychologist Carl Jung had a momentous impact on the writers of their generation.

The first fifteen years of the twentieth century witnessed unprecedented developments in technological fields. Radio became a major means of transmitting ideas to the public, in many instances replacing newspapers as the major news medium. The public was becoming more informed than ever before. Educational opportunities were available to growing numbers of people, causing a substantial increase in the size and nature of the reading public.

World Wars and Depression. The period between 1914 and 1945 was tumultuous. Both Canada and the United States mobilized for two world wars in only three decades. In the years between these wars, a period of freewheeling prosperity during the 1920s was followed by a worldwide economic depression that began in 1929 and was unparalleled in the history of either country.

After World War I, Paris became a gathering place for many North American writers and artists. The impressionism that flourished in the visual arts in Paris in the 1920s was reflected in all the arts. Much writing became experimental, as reflected very early in works such as Gertrude Stein's *Three Lives* (1909) and later in *The Making of Americans* (1925). Ernest Hemingway, following Stein's lead, developed a unique writing style, clipped and abbreviated, suggestive of the early poetry of the Imagist and vorticist poets, who focused on single objects and sought to capture and communicate their essences as sharply and succinctly as possible.

The Great Depression lasted from 1929 until 1940, when North America's new wartime economy brought about greater prosperity. While F. Scott Fitzgerald had depicted the high-flying 1920s in *The Great Gatsby* (1925), John Steinbeck was equally accurate in depicting the horrors of the economic meltdown of the 1930s in such novels as *Of Mice and Men* (1937) and *The Grapes of Wrath* (1939).

During the 1920s, the Harlem Renaissance brought many African American writers to public attention, among them Langston Hughes and Arna Bontemps. They paved the way for such later writers as Lorraine Hansberry, James Baldwin, Maya Angelou, Gwendolyn Brooks, and Nikki Giovanni.

After World War II. The period between the end of World War II and the early 1960s was one of relative calm, although the Korean War intruded upon it and resulted in substantial casualties on both sides. John Hersey had shown the horrors of nuclear war in his documentary book *Hiroshima* (1946), while his novel *A Bell for Adano* (1944) showed the more human side of war.

Drama flourished during this period with the arrival on Broadway of Tennessee Williams's *The Glass Menagerie* (1945), followed in quick succession by *A Streetcar Named Desire* (1947), *Summer and Smoke* (1948), and *Cat on a Hot Tin Roof* (1955). Arthur Miller's *All My Sons* (1947) tweaked the public conscience by depicting financial skulduggery among wartime businessmen. His greatest play, *Death of a Salesman* (1949), quickly became enshrined as a classic of American theater.

Social Unrest in the 1960s. The crucial change that led to the social unrest of the 1960s was the engagement of the United States in the Vietnam War. During this war, which many Americans considered unjust and unwarranted, thousands of draft-age Americans fled to Canada to avoid military service. The war dragged on for nearly a decade and divided a nation already stunned by the assassinations of President John F. Kennedy in 1963, and both Martin Luther King, Jr., and Robert Kennedy in 1968. Timothy O'Brien has written stirringly about the Vietnam War. His novel *If I Die in a Combat Zone, Box Me Up and Ship Me Home* (1973) established him as one of the foremost commentators on that war. Bob Dylan responded to the events of the 1960s and 1970s with his politically charged song lyrics.

The Focus on Social Issues. National discontent ran high as the 1960s neared their end.

African Americans demanded an end to segregation and to unequal treatment in the work place, in education, and in social services. Pride in being members of racial minorities grew as many of those on the fringes of society learned more about the heritage of their people. Toni Morrison, who in 1993 became the first African American woman to receive a Nobel Prize in Literature, celebrated her heritage in novels such as *The Bluest Eye* (1970), *Song of Solomon* (1977), and *Beloved* (1987), which focus on the strength of African American women.

Maya Angelou wrote about problems of incest and child abuse in her autobiographical novels *I Know Why the Caged Bird Sings* (1970) and *Gather Together in My Name* (1974). Gwendolyn Brooks celebrated the lives of the urban poor, particularly of African American women in Chicago, in both her poetry and prose written during the 1970s and 1980s.

In *Silent Dancing* (1990) and *The Latin Deli* (1993), Latina writer Judith Ortiz Cofer relates what it is like for a young Puerto Rican girl to be transplanted to New Jersey, where she lived through the winters of her formative years. Julia Alvarez from the Dominican Republic writes with equal feeling and considerable wit about her similar transplantation in *How the Garcia Girls Lost Their Accents* (1991). Alvarez's novel *In the Time of the Butterflies* (1994) recounts in chilling detail the excesses of the regime of Dominican dictator Rafael Trujillo.

Joan Didion examines another aspect of North American culture in her novels, frequently focusing on the underbelly of California culture. She often considers abortion, both literal and figurative, in her novels. In the book that many consider her best, *Democracy* (1984), she is centrally interested in presenting the aborted past and projecting an aborted future.

Looking Ahead. The literature of the twenty-first century will likely be much more technologically oriented than that of the twentieth century. Nevertheless, it probably will deal with the concerns of earlier eras, such as love, death, marriage, and personal loyalty; migrations of people into new territories, including space, evoking memories of such earlier writers as Willa Cather and Robertson Davies; questions of gender equality much like those touched on earlier by Margaret Atwood, Adrienne Rich, and Joan Didion; matters relating to racial or religious discrimination, as reflected earlier in the writings of Richard Wright, James Baldwin, Zora Neale Hurston, and Paul Lawrence Dunbar; and questions relating to the new wave of immigrants from other cultures, like those earlier presented by Isaac Bashevis Singer, Judith Ortiz Cofer, Julia Alvarez, and Chaim Potok.

Great American Writers: Twentieth Century provides rich background material for those who wish to broaden both their literary and their social horizons. Its list of selected authors is representative of the course that North American literature took through the twentieth century.

Organization of the Encyclopedia. As in most encyclopedias, articles are arranged alphabetically. Moreover, a uniform format is followed within every article, all of which are illustrated with full-color artwork. Each article begins with a summary of vital facts about an author, followed by a brief statement of the writer's place and significance in American literature. Next comes "The Writer's Life," an extended discussion of the most important events in the writer's life. Each section includes a lengthy time line summarizing events in the author's life.

"The Writer's Life" is followed by another long section titled "The Writer's Work," which focuses on the literary contributions of each author. This section deals with such matters as issues the authors raise in their writing, their recurrent themes, how they develop their characters, and other relevant matters. This section also includes a select bibliography, a sidebar on important inspirations in the writer's life, and lists of major publications.

The third section, "Reader's Guide to Major Works," deals at length with two or three of each author's most notable and representative published works. Essays relating to each title are followed by a list of sources for further study about that literary work. Each title discussed in this section is viewed in the light of themes, issues, and plot and is analyzed extensively.

The next section, "Other Works," summarizes briefly other writings by each author.

Finally, a list of resources follows each essay, providing information about Web sites about the author, manuscript collections of the author's work, societies devoted to studying him or her, and other important material that will help point the way for those who wish to pursue further study of that author.

R. BAIRD SHUMAN, GENERAL EDITOR

Contributors

Thomas P. Adler
Department of English, Purdue University

A. Owen Aldridge
Department of Comparative Literature, University of Illinois

Andrew J. Angyal
Department of English, Elon College

Jack Asker
Pasadena, California

Philip Bader
Pasadena, California

Jim Baird
Department of English, University of North Texas

Henry J. Baron
Department of English, Calvin College

Alvin K. Benson
Department of Geology, Brigham Young University

Milton Berman
Department of History, University of Rochester

Margaret Boe Birns
Division of Arts, Sciences & Humanities, New York University

Nicholas Birns
Department of Humanities, New School University

Pegge Bochynski
Beverly, Massachusetts

Bernadette Lynn Bosky
Yonkers, New York

Gerhard Brand
Department of English and Comparative Literature, California State University, Los Angeles, Professor Emeritus

C. K. Breckenridge
St. Louis, Missouri

Wesley Britton
Department of English, Harrisburg Area Community College

Edmund J. Campion
Department of Romance Languages, University of Tennessee

Mary LeDonne Cassidy
Department of English, South Carolina State University

Thomas J. Cassidy
Department of English, South Carolina State University

C. L. Chua
Department of English, California State University, Fresno

David W. Cole
Department of English, University of Wisconsin Colleges

John J. Conlon
Department of English, The University of Massachusetts, Boston

Frank Day
Department of English, Clemson University

M. Casey Diana
Department of English, University of Illinois, Urbana-Champaign

Joyce Duncan
Department of English, East Tennessee State University

Stefan R. Dziemianowicz
Bloomfield, New Jersey

Rebecca Hendrick Flannagan
Department of English, Francis Marion University

Robert J. Forman
Department of English, St. John's University

Ann D. Garbett
Department of English, Averett College

Joseph W. Hinton
Portland, Oregon

John R. Holmes
Department of English, Franciscan University of Steubenville

Joan Hope
Northborough, Massachusetts

Eric Howard
Los Angeles, California

Theodore C. Humphrey
Department of English and Foreign Languages, California State Polytechnic University, Pomona

Fiona Kelleghan
Otto G. Richter Library, University of Miami (Florida)

Claire Keyes
Department of English, Salem State College, Professor Emeritus

William T. Lawlor
Department of English, University of Wisconsin, Stevens Point

Leon Lewis
Department of English, Appalachian State University

R. C. Lutz
Department of English, University of the Pacific

Charles E. May
Department of English, Long Beach State University

Janet McCann
Department of English, Texas A & M University

Joanne McCarthy
  Tacoma, Washington
Ron McFarland
  Department of English, University of Idaho
Bernard E. Morris
  Modesto, California
Sherry Morton-Mollo
  Department of English, California State University, Fullerton
Robert J. Paradowski
  College of Liberal Arts, Rochester Institute of Technology
Margaret E. Parks
  Hale Library, Kansas State University
David Peck
  Department of English, California State University, Long Beach
Maureen J. Puffer-Rothenberg
  Odum Library, Valdosta State University
Rosemary M. Canfield Reisman
  Department of English, Charleston Southern University
Mark Rich
  Stevens Point, Wisconsin
Stephen R. Rohde
  Los Angeles, California

Carl Rollyson
  School of Liberal Arts & Sciences, The City University of New York, Baruch College, Associate Dean
Joseph Rosenblum
  Department of English, University of North Carolina, Greensboro
Kelly Rothenberg
  Valdosta, Georgia
Carroll Dale Short
  Birmingham, Alabama
R. Baird Shuman
  Department of English, University of Illinois
August W. Staub
  Department of Drama, University of Georgia
Christine D. Tomei
  Slavic Seminar, Columbia University
Ronald G. Walker
  Department of English, Western Illinois University
Kathryn A. Walterscheid
  Department of English, University of Missouri, St. Louis
Melanie Watkins
  Pasadena, California
Michael Witkoski
  Columbia, South Carolina

Contents

James Agee

BORN: November 27, 1909, Knoxville, Tennessee
DIED: May 16, 1955, New York, New York
IDENTIFICATION: Mid-twentieth-century journalist, poet, novelist, film critic. Wrote movie scripts and screenplays, several of which were made into classic American films.

Agee was best known in his lifetime for the essay *Let Us Now Praise Famous Men* (1941) and the posthumously published novel *A Death in the Family* (1957). However, he also explored other genres, publishing many poems, some of which have been set to music. In all genres, he was a poetic writer whose sensibilities went against the grain of the current American society. His unique documentary work with photographer Walker Evans, *Let Us Now Praise Famous Men*, is a highly detailed, personal record of the lives of tenant farm families. It was virtually ignored in its time but was later recognized as an enduring social history. Agee is credited with creating the genre of film criticism, being its first serious literary critic. His screenplays for *The African Queen* (1951) and *The Night of the Hunter* (1955) were made into films that are now American classics. At the time of his death none of his works was still in print; however, he has since been recognized as a brilliant and unique artist.

The Writer's Life

James Rufus Agee was born on November 27, 1909, in the small Tennessee city of Knoxville. He was the first child and only son of Hugh James Agee, a businessman from a family in the southern rural mountain country of Tennessee, and Laura Tyler Agee, a pious Episcopalian from an educated northern family. His parents' differing social backgrounds and religious sensibilities created great emotional conflict in Agee. His exploration of religious feeling and social conscience became the basis for his most artistically successful work.

Childhood. Called Rufus by his family, James Agee was a sensitive, intelligent boy. His early childhood was secure and happy until the death of his father in a car accident when Agee was six years old. After the death of his father, to whom he was especially close, Agee moved with his mother and sister onto the grounds of St. Andrew's School, an Episcopal preparatory boarding school in the Cumberland Mountains of south-central Tennessee. He attended St. Andrew's from 1919 until 1924, living a lonely life in a dormitory. At St. Andrew's, he met Father James Harold Flye, who became his friend and surrogate father, providing guidance and inspiration throughout Agee's tempestuous life.

Education. In 1924 Agee entered the exclusive Phillips Exeter Academy in Exeter, New Hampshire, where his interest in writing developed. He edited the school's paper, the *Phillips Exeter Monthly*, and his writing flourished. In 1928 he entered Harvard University, further proving his talents by writing poetry and short stories. He was always a populist with a great compassion for the disadvantaged, and he kept his distance from the elite world of Harvard. A person of true artistic temperament, he suffered through episodes of severe depression and heavy drinking. These never seemed to interfere with his growing literary output but would eventually ruin his health. In the summer of 1929, he spent several months working as a day laborer in the Midwest, an experience that provided material he would return to in future stories.

The Journalist. After graduating from Harvard in 1932, Agee went to work for *Fortune* magazine as a reporter. He was never comfortable writing for a magazine that glorified wealth and material success, so he often wrote anonymously; however, the job allowed him freedom to work on personal writing projects. In 1934 he published *Permit Me Voyage*, a volume of poetry that

A promotion for a motorcycle shop in Agee's hometown of Knoxville, Tennessee, in 1915, the same year Agee's father died in an automobile accident.

received generally good reviews. Reviewers praised the rhythm of his work and his sensitivity in rendering detail. However, he was unable to focus his energy and talents on one literary form and soon turned to prose.

In 1936 Agee and photographer Walker Evans were assigned by *Fortune* to write a documentary on the lives of sharecroppers in Alabama during the Great Depression. Living with these families affected Agee deeply. Although the work that Agee and Walker created was rejected by *Fortune*, Agee spent several years revising it. The result was *Let Us Now Praise Famous Men*—a long, passionately detailed account of the hardships and beauty in the lives of three desperately poor families. In 1936 Agee also wrote "Knoxville: Summer of 1915," a sketch that evokes childhood memories of summer evenings in his hometown. Considered among his best fiction writing, it would become the prologue for his most touching work, the autobiographical *A Death in the Family*. In 1937 Agee's four-year marriage to Olivia Saunders ended, and he began a relationship with Alma Mailman.

The Film Critic and Screenwriter. Agee
had a special passion for films. In 1938, while still working on *Let Us Now Praise Famous Men*, he began writing book and film reviews for *Time* magazine. He and Alma married in 1939, and a son, Joel, was born in 1941. Agee was apparently unsuited for the restrictions of marriage, however; Alma left him shortly after Joel was born. Agee continued his obsessive pace of constant work, sleepless nights, and heavy smoking and drinking, seemingly on a course of self-destruction. In 1942 he began writing a film review column for the *Nation* in addition to his work for *Time*, and he continued writing prolifically for both magazines until 1948.

Agee supported himself as a journalist throughout the 1940s. In 1946 he was married for the third time, to Mia Fritsch, with whom he had three children. Always restless, he began to write screenplays for films instead of just writing about them. He began a successful career as a screenwriter, but his addictions to

Agee in a photograph taken by his friend Helen Levitt in 1945. While Agee was trying to find his niche as a writer, Levitt had already become the first female photographer to have a one-woman show at the Museum of Modern Art in New York.

tobacco and alcohol began to take a toll. Agee suffered his first heart attack in 1951, the same year in which his collaboration with director John Huston produced the film *The African Queen*. Agee's novella, *The Morning Watch*, was also published in that year, as his health continued to decline.

In spite of his worsening health, the early 1950s were productive and artistically successful for Agee. He worked on television programs, scripts and screenplays, and in 1955 his adaptation of the novel *The Night of the Hunter* became a popular film. In the midst of his artistic productivity, Agee suffered another serious heart attack. On May 16, 1955, James Agee died in a taxi on the way to his doctor's office. He was forty-five years old.

HIGHLIGHTS IN AGEE'S LIFE

1909   James Rufus Agee is born on November 27, in Knoxville, Tennessee.

1915   Agee's father, Hugh James Agee, is killed in an automobile accident.

1919–1924 Agee attends St. Andrew's Episcopal School in Tennessee; forms lifelong friendship with Father James Harold Flye.

1924–1928 Attends Phillips Exeter Academy, Exeter, New Hampshire; edits the *Phillips Exeter Monthly*.

1929   Spends summer as a day laborer and harvest hand in Midwest.

1928–1932 Attends Harvard University; edits *The Advocate*.

1932   Begins work as a journalist at *Fortune* magazine.

1933   Marries Olivia Saunders.

1935   Takes leave of absence from *Fortune* to work on personal writing projects.

1936   Returns to *Fortune*; writes story on sharecroppers that is rejected by *Fortune*.

1937   Marriage to Olivia ends; Agee forms relationship with Alma Mailman.

1939   Leaves *Fortune*; begins reviewing films for *Time* magazine; marries Alma.

1941   Finally publishes sharecropper story as *Let Us Now Praise Famous Men*; son Joel is born; Alma leaves Agee.

1942–1948 Writes weekly film column for the *Nation*.

1946   Marries Mia Fritsch; daughter Julia Teresa is born.

1948   Writes narration for documentary film *The Quiet One*.

1951   Publishes *The Morning Watch*; collaborates with John Huston on script for *The African Queen*; suffers first heart attack.

1955   *The Night of the Hunter* becomes a popular film; dies of a heart attack on May 16.

1957   *A Death in the Family* is published unfinished with revisions made by editors.

1958   *A Death in the Family* is awarded a posthumous Pulitzer Prize for best fiction.

The Writer's Work

James Agee wrote two novels, many short stories, experimental nonfiction, poetry, movie reviews, scripts, and screenplays. A poetic writer whose sensibilities went against the grain of American society while he was alive, he was best known during his lifetime as a journalist and film critic. He is now most remembered and admired for his autobiographical novel *A Death in the Family*, as well as his unique documentary work with photographer Walker Evans, *Let Us Now Praise Famous Men*. Their highly detailed, personal record of the lives of tenant farm families was virtually ignored in its time but was later recognized as an enduring social history.

The Restless Writer. Agee's poetic, spiritual, and emotional style reflects his sensitive and passionate nature. His intense awareness of the fleeting and fragile nature of human life is deeply felt in all of his work, including his objective reporting as a journalist. The effects of his father's tragic early death and a sense of longing and loneliness pervade his writing. In addition, Agee felt the weight of his Christian upbringing as a web of deep conflicts, which he explored eloquently in his autobiographical fiction.

Observation and documentation were Agee's passions, and he realized that his own experience would provide his best material. An example of his best prose, the sketch

"Knoxville: Summer of 1915" is a fictional account of summer evenings Agee remembered from childhood, recalling an atmosphere and an unspoken feeling of special time with his family. Much of the power of his writing comes from his ability to perceive and describe reality, to re-create conversations and the actual atmosphere of a place and time. Agee's capacity for observing and rendering fine detail and complex emotion were not limited to fiction and reporting, however. In 1934 he published *Permit Me Voyage*, a book of poetry that received good reviews.

Agee and Film. Agee is considered by many to be the first serious American reviewer of popular film, essentially establishing film criticism as a new literary genre. From his youth, he was passionately interested in every aspect

The loneliness and isolation experienced by the six-year-old Agee as a result of his father's sudden death are reflected in the 1937 oil painting *Connecticut Autumn* by O. Louis Guglielmi. Agee's loss is the foundation for his Pulitzer Prize–winning novel, *A Death in the Family*.

Actors Katharine Hepburn and Humphrey Bogart in the classic motion picture *The African Queen.* Agee wrote the screenplay with director John Huston in 1951.

of cinema and filmmaking, and he began writing film reviews in 1939. He contributed prolifically to the literature of film, as a reviewer, screenwriter, and proponent of the social and ethical responsibilities of all artists. He believed that movies should serve social as well as artistic purposes and set high standards for the films he reviewed, as well as for those he created.

Beginning in the late 1940s, Agee used his observation for detail to write screenplays in which words, images, and sound perfectly supported one another. He wrote the narration for *The Quiet One* (1948), a film documentary about a troubled young boy in Harlem. He also wrote commercial scripts, adapting several novels and short stories. In the early 1950s Agee wrote the scripts or screenplays for seven films, many of which were produced. He collaborated with director John Huston, adapting C. S. Forester's novel *The African Queen* (1935) for the screen. His screenplay received an Academy Award nomination, and the film became a beloved classic. Agee's career as a screenwriter was artistically and financially successful and personally fulfilling.

Inspired and Self-Destructive. Agee worked continuously, writing fiction as well as scripts and screenplays, and adapting scripts for television. His modest novella, *The Morning Watch*, was published in 1951, receiving mixed reviews. He continued to work on an autobiographical novel about a father's death and a boy's memories of his family, which would become *A Death in the Family*. Published after his death, this novel received a Pulitzer Prize for fiction in 1958.

Agee suffered a heart attack in 1951 and was advised by his doctor to slow his pace, which he was characteristically unable to do. Restless and driven, he continued drinking heavily and working feverishly on scripts and screenplays. In 1952 he suffered another serious heart attack. In the same year, Agee wrote the screenplay, from a story by Stephen Crane, for the film *The Bride Comes to Yellow Sky*; it is considered among Agee's best screenplays. He also had a small acting role in the film. Agee's 1955 adaptation of Davis Grubb's 1953 novel *The Night of the Hunter* became one of cinema's most frightening and compelling films.

BIBLIOGRAPHY

Bergreen, Lawrence. *James Agee: A Life.* New York: Dutton, 1984.

Kramer, Victor A. *Agee and Actuality: Artistic Vision in His Work.* Troy, N.Y.: Whitston, 1991.

———. *James Agee.* Boston: Twayne Publishers, 1975.

Lofaro, Michael A., ed. *James Agee: Some Reconsiderations.* Knoxville: University of Tennessee Press, 1992.

Lowe, James. *The Creative Process of James Agee.* Baton Rouge: Louisiana State University Press, 1994.

MacLeish, Archibald. Foreword to *Permit Me Voyage.* New Haven, Conn.: Yale University Press, 1934.

Madden, David, ed. *Remembering James Agee.* 2d ed. Athens: University of Georgia Press, 1997.

Neuman, Alma. *Always Straight Ahead: A Memoir.* Baton Rouge: Louisiana State University Press, 1993.

Snyder, John J. *James Agee: A Study of His Film Criticism.* New York: Arno Press, 1977.

Spiegel, Alan. *James Agee and the Legend of Himself: A Critical Study.* Columbia: University of Missouri Press, 1998.

LONG FICTION

1951   The Morning Watch
1957   A Death in the Family

SHORT FICTION

1952   "A Mother's Tale"
1964   Four Early Stories by James Agee
1968   The Collected Short Prose of James Agee

POETRY

1934   Permit Me Voyage
1968   The Collected Poems of James Agee

SCREENPLAYS

1951   The Red Badge of Courage (based on Stephen Crane's novel)
1951   The African Queen (based on C. S. Forester's novel)
1952   The Bride Comes to Yellow Sky (based on Crane's short story)
1953   Noa Noa
1953   White Mane
1955   Green Magic
1955   The Night of the Hunter
1960   Agee on Film: Five Film Scripts

NONFICTION

1941   Let Us Now Praise Famous Men (with photographs by Walker Evans)
1958   Agee on Film: Reviews and Comments
1962   Letters of James Agee to Father Flye
1985   Selected Journalism, ed. Paul Ashdown

Reader's Guide to Major Works

A DEATH IN THE FAMILY

Genre: Fiction
Subgenre: Semi-autobiographical novel
Published: New York, 1957
Time period: Four days in 1915
Setting: Knoxville, Tennessee

Themes and Issues. In even the most loving families, the death of a parent can shatter a child's life. This story is a record of a family's irreparable loss, and at the same time, a celebration of life and family love. After the tragic death of his father, six-year-old Rufus must suddenly cope with adult loneliness. For Rufus, a world that had seemed beautiful and comforting is now cold and frightening. He can no longer look to his adored father for comfort, and home will never again be the same for him.

The Plot. Six-year-old Rufus and his parents, Jay and Mary, return home after watching a Charlie Chaplin film together in town. During the night, Jay is awakened by a telephone call from his brother, asking him to come to the home of their father, who is critically ill. Before Jay drives to his father's home in the mountains, he tells his wife he will try to be home by the following evening, before the children go to bed.

The next day, Rufus's mother's Aunt Hannah buys Rufus a cap, which he loves. That evening, Mary receives a call informing her that Jay has had a serious accident. She calls her brother,

Alexandre Hogue's 1934 oil-on-canvas painting *Drouth Stricken Area* (Dallas Museum of Art) depicts the infertility of the land and the loss of animal life that resulted in the extreme poverty of many farmers throughout the Great Depression of the 1930s.

SOME INSPIRATIONS BEHIND AGEE'S WORK

The most profound influences on James Agee's work are found in his childhood and youth in Tennessee. The early accidental death of his father forever altered Agee's happy and stable family; the sudden and senseless tragedy left him intensely lonely and very sad, searching for a comforting explanation of his family's loss.

Agee's mother's religious fervor and his own Christian education helped form his strong moral conscience, which he felt as a great weight. The conflicts arising from his Christian education created immense guilt in Agee but also gave him a strong moral foundation. He believed that all artists have a responsibility toward humanity. The virtuous and compassionate desire to alleviate suffering inspired some of his most compelling soul searching and is at the heart of his masterpiece, *Let Us Now Praise Famous Men*.

At the age of nine Agee met Father James Harold Flye, his history teacher at St. Andrew's School. A strong mutual bond of respect and affection was established. Although they did not see each other often after Agee left school, they corresponded for more than thirty years in lively letters full of ideas, discussions of books, and open, sincere friendship. Agee's letters to Father Flye were published in 1962.

who goes to the site of the accident, and returns to tell her that Jay's car went off the road and he was killed instantly. The accident is blamed on a mechanical problem, but it is clear that Jay often drank too much and drove too fast. Aunt Hannah and Mary's parents arrive to sit with her, and they mourn for Jay together.

Unaware of the events of the previous evening, Rufus gets up, expecting to find his adored father home, anxious to show him his new cap. His mother asks him to go get his sister, and she tells the children that their father will not be coming home, because he was badly hurt and God took him up to Heaven. Aunt Hannah gives the children many details of the accident, which Rufus does not fully understand, but which capture his imagination. In order to impress some boys who have teased him, he tells them the story of his father's death, which they have heard about in the newspaper. He is deeply ashamed of this later, but is proud that something so exciting has happened to his family.

As the family members prepare for Jay's funeral, they express their grief over his death and their interpretations of the event very differently. The children are not allowed to attend the funeral; instead they stay with a friend, who takes them up onto a nearby hill so they can watch from a distance. In the final scene, Mary's brother, who is bitter and nonreligious, tells Rufus about his father's funeral. He says that something almost "miraculous" happened, something which could make him almost believe in God. As the casket was lowered, he says, a butterfly landed on top of it. When the casket touched the ground, the butterfly flew high up into the sky, as if it were going to Heaven.

Analysis. Almost all of the characters in this novel are based on real people in James Agee's family. Agee conceived his most successful fictional piece as a "remembrance" of his childhood and a "memorial" to his father, who died in an accident when Agee was six. Agee is most successful in re-creating a small boy's percep-

Young Agee and his aunt lavish their affection on a pair of kittens.

tions of the adult world and the events going on around him. Agee feels that everyone is lonely, and he makes the reader feel that Rufus's loneliness is different from that of the adults. The father in Agee's work is idealized, both in life and in death. Agee and his father were close, and after his father's death, Agee was a "lost soul," longing for a God he still could believe in.

Although Agee worked on this piece for more than twenty years, it was left unfinished at the time of his death in 1955. The prologue, which had actually been completed in 1935, was added to the beginning of the novel by the editors who finished Agee's work for publication in 1957.

SOURCES FOR FURTHER STUDY

Barson, Alfred T. *A Way of Seeing: A Critical Study of James Agee*. Amherst: University of Massachusetts Press, 1972.

Doty, Mark A. *Tell Me Who I Am: James Agee's Search for Selfhood*. Baton Rouge: Louisiana State University Press, 1981.

Moss, Joyce, and George Wilson, eds. "James Agee: A Death in the Family." In *Growth of Empires to the Great Depression (1890–1930s)*. Vol. 3 in *Literature and Its Times: Profiles of 300 Notable Literary Works and the Historical Events That Influenced Them*. Detroit: Gale Research, 1997.

Seib, Kenneth. *A Death in the Family: A Critical Commentary*. New York: American R.D.M., 1965.

LET US NOW PRAISE FAMOUS MEN

Genre: Nonfiction
Subgenre: Documentary with accompanying photographs
Published: New York, 1941
Time period: Eight weeks during the summer of 1936
Setting: West-central Alabama

Themes and Issues. What began as a writing assignment while Agee was a journalist for Fortune magazine became a life-altering experience and provided the material for his literary masterpiece. Agee was critical of the dehumanizing aspects of modern mass urban culture, though it had brought him opportunities and success. His privileged background and education had not prepared him for the extreme poverty of the tenant farm families he lived with in Alabama. The idea that the magazine might publish a story about them to elicit pity from readers disgusted him; in the sharecroppers he found strong values and a beauty that was missing in contemporary modern life. A political leftist, Agee was highly sympathetic to labor and the workers and skeptical of the American capitalist economy that valued profit over the welfare of working people.

The Plot. Lacking a conventional plot, Agee's book records in intimate detail the day-to-day lives of three desperately poor families. In

1936 Agee and photographer Walker Evans were assigned by Fortune magazine to produce a social documentary examining the lives of white cotton sharecroppers, assessing the effectiveness of government aid to alleviate the social and economic trauma of the Great Depression of the 1930s. The Gudger, Ricketts, and Woods families allowed Agee and Evans to live with them for two months. They shared the families' food and slept on their floors, recording the details, textures, feelings, and sounds they experienced. Almost a confessional, *Let Us Now Praise Famous Men* began as a documentary and became a highly personal record in the hands of Agee and Evans. In part because it was so unconventional, it received generally poor reviews from critics and was ignored by readers.

Analysis. Steeped in Christian teachings, Agee questions the values of a modern culture in which people can live in utter squalor. Despite his privileged social background, his emotional roots were in the Tennessee soil. He had great empathy for poor working people, like those of his father's family, and he felt that he had betrayed his father's poor southern upbringing by becoming successful in the urban, literary culture of the North. Although Agee's artistic sensibilities create a deeply personal work of poetic language and imagery, he played down the work's artistic style. He wanted his work to reveal nature and truth as it really was. He

A farmhouse kitchen as seen through the lens of photographer Walker Evans. Evans and Agee collaborated in creating the documentary *Let Us Now Praise Famous Men*.

hoped his work would be read as a portrait of real people, as well as an emotional cry of despair for the common man.

The original work Agee and Evans produced in 1936 was rejected by *Fortune*. Its experimental style focused on real people, quite against the grain of the star-struck, glamour-loving culture of 1930s America. Agee's unorthodox use of punctuation, odd page layout, and frank descriptions of sexuality alarmed critics and repelled readers. Agee's revised, highly detailed, passionate, and poetic essay was finally published in 1941. Critics of *Let Us Now Praise Famous Men* see in it Agee's endless examination of his own motives and emotional conflicts, along with a search for identity in his fascination with and empathy for the smallest details of the sharecroppers' lives.

SOURCES FOR FURTHER STUDY

Macdonald, Dwight. *Against the American Grain*. New York: Random House, 1962.

Maharidge, Dale, et al. *And Their Children After Them: The Legacy of "Let Us Now Praise Famous Men," James Agee, Walker Evans, and the Rise and Fall of Cotton in the South*. New York: Pantheon, 1990.

Stott, William. *Documentary Expression and Thirties America*. Chicago: University of Chicago Press, 1986.

Ward, J. A. *American Silences: The Realism of James Agee, Walker Evans, and Edward Hopper*. Baton Rouge: Louisiana State University Press, 1985.

Agee's writing reflects a deep respect for the plight of sharecroppers. Marie Atchinson Hull's 1935 oil painting *Tenant Farmer* conveys the quiet truth, strength, and dignity Agee admired in hardworking people.

Other Works

THE MORNING WATCH (1951). Considered by many to be his least successful fiction, *The Morning Watch* was nevertheless praised as a sign of James Agee's potential skill as a writer. This novella concerns one day in the life of a sensitive twelve-year-old boy named Richard, a student at a religious boarding school. In its careful record of detail, *The Morning Watch* closely parallels Agee's experience. It explores the difficulties of sustaining religious faith, the fragility of human existence, and many other themes that pervade Agee's writing.

Richard is a student at a school much like St. Andrew's, which Agee attended from 1919 to 1924. Richard and his fellow students are anticipating the events of Maundy Thursday evening, the day before Good Friday, when Christ was resurrected. The students traditionally hold a vigil until the early hours of Good Friday, and it is a special time, filled with earnest excitement and the will to pray well.

All year Richard has looked forward to this day, and he has tried to be good in order to feel true religious emotion. His religious meditations are intruded upon, however, both by his own active, curious mind and by the youthful mischief of the other boys. After his prayer in the chapel, Richard and two other boys go swimming instead of returning to their dormitory. There, Richard fixates on an empty insect shell and begins to feel an awareness of the world around him. His thoughts lead him to consider the world of his senses, his intellect, and his observation of beauty, which stir in him his first feelings of skepticism toward his religious education. Richard finally has a sense of the fragility of all things. The purity of childhood and unquestioning faith begin to leave him, through a gradual change, and bring an awareness of suffering and death.

The Morning Watch has been criticized for its heavy reliance on obvious symbolism and an unsatisfying ending. However, it was also praised for its emotion and the moving depiction of sincere religious feeling and the changing awareness in a young boy.

Resources

A collection of James Agee's literary manuscripts and correspondence is housed in the Harry Ransom Humanities Research Center at the University of Texas at Austin. Other sources of information to students of Agee include the following:

James Agee Collection. The Harry Ransom Humanities Research Center's extensive James Agee holdings are cataloged in detail on line. The Web site also includes a biographical sketch, scope and contents of the collection, and an index of people with whom Agee corresponded. (http://www.lib.utexas.edu/hrc/fa/agee.james.html)

James Agee Film Project. An organization in Charlottesville, Virginia, that produces and distributes documentary films about James Agee and related issues. Video titles available include *Agee* (1978), *An Afternoon with Father Flye* (1984), and *To Render a Life* (1992). (http://www.ageefilms.org/agee.html)

Thomas Hampson: I Hear America Singing. In cooperation with the PBS broadcast network, Thirteen/WNET in New York produced this *Great Performances* special on the American Concert Song, which originally aired in 1997. The Web companion piece to the PBS program features an extensively documented series of sites, linking James Agee's twentieth-century poetry to the early American Romanticists of the 1800s. There is specific biographical and critical information on James Agee, as well as samples of his poetry set to music. (http://www.pbs.org/wnet/ihas/)

The American Experience: Let Us Now Praise Famous Men-Revisited. This sixty-minute documentary, produced by WETA-TV in 1988, retraces the path that writer James Agee and photographer Walker Evans followed in 1936 for their book.

MARGARET E. PARKS

Julia Alvarez

BORN: March 27, 1950, New York, New York
IDENTIFICATION: Late twentieth-century Dominican American writer
of poems, essays, short stories, and novels.

Julia Alvarez's novels, stories, poems, and essays are critically acclaimed for
the depth and sensitivity of her treatment of the expatriate theme. As a Latina,
bicultural and bilingual, she explores how individuals adapt to new cultures,
learn new languages, and face forces of oppression and despotism with
courage and resolve. Her work argues that language weaves the web of life,
knitting together the stories of the family's journey, the choices, conflicts, tri-
umphs, and disappointments for the expatriate writer in particular. Because
her work examines the challenges facing all expatriates, the Dominican
American community and the public generally have praised her work.

The Writer's Life

Julia Altagracia María Teresa Alvarez was born on March 27, 1950, in New York City but returned with her family to the Dominican Republic when she was three weeks old. She lived there for ten years with her large extended family of aunts, uncles, and many cousins. Her family on her mother's side was wealthy, and her father was a successful physician. Therefore, she grew up in considerable luxury. Her father was the twenty-fifth legitimate child of his father, and he had an unknown number of illegitimate half brothers and half sisters. Alvarez's family, as she writes, was therefore messy and complicated but also full of stories, family dinners, and vacations.

In other respects, however, life in the Dominican Republic became increasingly tense under the dictatorship of Generalísimo Rafael Leónidas Trujillo Molina, who ruled the country for over thirty years beginning in 1930. Alvarez's father, part of a plot to overthrow Trujillo, escaped with his immediate family from the Dominican Republic in August of 1960. The family moved into permanent exile in the United States, where Alvarez's father eventually established a successful medical practice and continued to support his family in an upper-middle-class manner.

Childhood. The second of four daughters, Alvarez was surrounded in her early childhood by a large traditional family in which the men went off to work while the women stayed home, surrounded by servants, and tended to the business of child rearing. As Alvarez and her three sisters entered their turbulent teenage years in New York City at the height of the 1960s, they chafed at the pressures of their extended family and the particularly female responsibility to guard the family secrets.

The Future Writer. Alvarez turned early to literature, deciding as a child that she wanted to be a poet. Her grandfather, who often recited poetry, gave his blessing to this ambition. However, for her first ten years, the English language, which her parents used to discuss matters such as politics and sex, which they did not want the children to hear, was the "sound of worry and secrets, the sound of being left out." Alvarez became intrigued with idiomatic language, both English and Spanish, becoming profoundly fascinated with the magic of poetry. A sixth-grade teacher, Sister Maria Generosa, nurtured Alvarez's love of language, but her growing mastery of English came at the price of speaking Spanish with an accent. Frequent visits to the Dominican Republic as a teenager after the overthrow of Trujillo made her realize that she was a linguistic outsider in her homeland, a concept that became a major thread in her poetry, fiction, and essays, despite her fluency in both languages and cultures.

Education. Before her move to the United States, Alvarez attended the Carol Morgan School, founded by Carol Morgan, an American missionary and a friend of her grandmother, in the Dominican Republic. After moving to the United States, she attended public schools, a Catholic school, and then a New England boarding school, the Abbot Academy. She attended Connecticut College from 1967 to 1969, when she transferred to Middlebury College. She earned her bachelor's degree summa cum laude from Middlebury in 1971. Her graduate studies at Syracuse University earned her a master's degree in creative writing in 1975. She attended The Bread Loaf Writers' Conference from 1979 to 1980 before committing herself to becoming a writer.

The Fledgling Writer. As a child, Julia often hid under her bed to avoid going to school. While hiding, she would immerse herself in

The Alvarez family's move from the Dominican Republic to New York City offered promise, excitement, sorrow, and an introduction to the English language. Bilingualism remains a major theme of Alvarez's writing. The breadth and diversity of New York culture are reflected in Malcah Zeldis's painting *Times Square*.

HIGHLIGHTS IN ALVAREZ'S LIFE

1950	Julia Alvarez is born in New York City, March 27, 1950.
1950–1960	Lives in the Dominican Republic, until fleeing with family to the United States.
1967	Graduates from the Abbot Academy.
1967–1969	Attends Connecticut College.
1971	Receives bachelor's degree from Middlebury College.
1975	Receives master's degree in creative writing from Syracuse University.
1975–1977	Conducts poetry workshops in schools, prisons, and nursing homes for the Kentucky Arts Commission.
1978	Works for the National Endowment for the Arts in poetry programs in Delaware and North Carolina.
1979	Coedits *Old Age Ain't for Sissies*, a collection of poetry by North Carolina senior citizens.
1979–1980	Attends Bread Loaf Writers' Conference in Middlebury, Vermont.
1979–1981	Teaches English at Phillips Andover Academy in Andover, Massachusetts.
1981	Awarded summer residency in fiction from Yaddo, a writers' colony in Saratoga Springs, New York.
1981–1983	Visiting assistant professor of creative writing at University of Vermont, Burlington.
1984–1985	Jenny McKean Moore Visiting Writer at George Washington University in Washington, D.C.
1984	Publishes *Homecoming: Poems*, her first book of poems.
1985–1988	Assistant professor of English at the University of Illinois, Urbana.
1988	Begins teaching literature and creative writing at Middlebury College.
1989	Marries Bill Eichner.
1991	Publishes first novel, *How the Garcia Girls Lost Their Accents*.
1994	Publishes *In the Time of the Butterflies*.
1995	Publishes *The Other Side: El Otro Lado*, a book of poems.
1996	Reissues *Homecoming: New and Collected Poems*.
1997	Publishes *¡Yo!*, a novel.
1998	Is appointed writer-in-residence at Middlebury College.
1998	Publishes *Something to Declare*, a book of essays, and *Seven Trees*, a book of poems.
2000	Publishes *The Secret Footprints*, a children's book.

stories from *The Arabian Nights; Entertainments*, the only voluntary reading she did as a child, learning from Scheherazade that one could be saved by telling stories. Alvarez's writing talent was also nurtured by her family's skill for and habit of storytelling. The oral tradition of her homeland gave her a strong background for her writing, and her new American teachers encouraged her to write down her memories of the Dominican world.

In the late 1970s Alvarez began to publish poetry, essays, and short fiction. In 1979 she coedited and published *Old Age Ain't for Sissies*, an anthology of poetry written by senior citizens in creative writing workshops that she ran in North Carolina. She became increasingly prolific in all three genres throughout the 1980s and 1990s. *Homecoming: Poems* (1984) was a handmade book of her housekeeping poems, parts of which she wrote while at Yaddo, the writers' colony where she began to discover her voice as a woman and as a Latina. Her first novel, *How the García Girls Lost Their Accents* (1991), was followed by *In the Time of the Butterflies* (1994), *The Other Side: El Otro Lado* (1995), a book of poems; *Homecoming: New and Collected Poems* (1996); her third novel, *¡Yo!* (1997); *Seven Trees* (1998), another book of poems; and *Something to Declare* (1998), a book of essays.

Academic Life. After earning her master's degree, Alvarez taught writing from 1975 to 1985, mostly as an adjunct teacher in a number of different contexts ranging from state arts commissions to Phillips Andover Academy to the University of Illinois. From 1988 to 1998 she taught English at Middlebury College, Middlebury, Vermont. In 1998 the special position of writer-in-residence was created for her at Middlebury.

Marriage and Domestic Life. The imprint of *la familia* (a widely extended family) and of the Dominican culture in Alvarez's life and work remains indelible. She married her third husband, ophthalmologist Bill Eichner, on June 3, 1989, and the couple moved to a farm near Middlebury, Vermont. This union provided Alvarez with a significant sense of psychological security and marked the beginning of an intensely productive period of her life.

This publicity photograph of Alvarez, date unknown, was used to promote at least three of her books.

The Writer's Work

Julia Alvarez is known for writing poetry, long and short fiction, essays, and children's books. Her work explores themes of language, culture, and the tradition of storytelling in which she was raised.

Issues in Alvarez's Fiction. The nature and function of writing are major issues for Alvarez; therefore, her work constantly explores the nature and function of storytelling and stories and the roles stories play for the individual and for the larger community. In her collection of essays, *Something to Declare*, she argues that storytelling creates community, and, in telling and knowing "the secret heart of each other's lives," it decreases individuals' isolation. The last lines of *¡Yo!* emphasize how family stories tell of the journey to the present. The entire novel is metafiction, a fictional form that examines every aspect of creative writing, including its emotional challenges, as well as the writer's need for love and acceptance and the writer's transforming of experience into art.

In all of Alvarez's work, stories create the fabric and truth of her characters' lives. They also serve to create a lasting memory of peoples' lives. In the historical fiction *In the Time of the Butterflies*, the story of the Mirabal sisters is created from the fragments of oral legend and history, memorializing their courage and warning against the dangers of dictatorships. Alvarez argues consistently in her fiction and poetry that writing matters because it takes writers out of themselves and into the lives and worlds of others, knitting individuals together as a human species. At the same time, writers must struggle to find their own voices, however difficult that process might be.

A second major theme in Alvarez's work is feminism and the rejection of the macho tradition of male domination. The issue is complex because the cultural traditions of gender and class-based sexual behaviors are deeply ingrained in her female, as well as her male, characters. In the traditional Catholic society of the Dominican Republic, sexual activity is seen on one level as an important privilege to be enjoyed only within the sanctity of marriage; therefore, the pressures to marry are enormous. However, Dominican men have traditionally maintained extramarital liaisons,

The negative effects of machismo, often explored in Alvarez's writing, are reflected in Francis Picabia's 1922 *La Nuit Espagnole* (*The Spanish Night*).

SOME INSPIRATIONS BEHIND ALVAREZ'S WORK

In *Something to Declare*, Alvarez writes that she sees her writing as multilayered, and that underneath the more obvious influences, such as George Eliot, Toni Morrison, Emily Dickinson, Maxine Hong Kingston, and Sandra Cisneros, are other real-life women who "traipsed into my imagination with broom and dusting rag, cookbook and garden scissors, Gladys and the aunts, the cook at Yaddo and her sidekick, the lady with the vacuum cleaner."

Alvarez's most fundamental indebtedness, however, is to her large and verbal extended Dominican family, that swirl of aunts and uncles, of grandparents, cousins, and sisters, of maids and neighbors. All these people told and corrected stories about each other. The maids, especially the pantry maid, Gladys, taught her songs, folk remedies, and the secrets of life of which they were the keepers. The seed for her writing was planted in the Dominican soil and nourished by teachers in her English classes in New York as well as by the example of other bilingual, bicultural writers such as William Carlos Williams, Maxine Hong Kingston, Sandra Cisneros, Rudolpho Anaya, and Gary Soto. The sounds and rhythms of that second language, the English spoken in New York City, was an additional influence.

keeping many women in abused and subjected states. There is a tension in Alvarez's work between her female characters' intense desire for love and security and their feminist opposition to a traditional and hypocritical male view of protecting the virginity of daughters while engaging in illicit affairs. Alvarez writes honestly about the presence and the pressures of these issues in her characters' lives: The three García sisters all make poor marriage choices, and the Mirabal women discover that their father has a secret second family.

The most significant issue in Alvarez's work is the bicultural, bilingual experience as both personal problem and rich resource. Alvarez frequently explores the reconciliation of the often conflicting claims of her two cultures and her two languages. She seeks, in her writing to claim the integrity of her total experience. Writing is, for Alvarez, a way to integrate her two cultures within the homeland of language, to take and display both the "nativeness" and the "foreignness" of her experience and turn it into art—and truth. She hopes to create, as she writes in *Something to Declare*, "a literature that will widen and enrich the existing canon." She writes in English because it is the language in which she was trained to write. She knows the heft and feel of English grammar and rhetoric much more completely than that of Spanish. However, as a Spanish speaker, she does not "hear the same rhythms in English as a native speaker of English." She seeks to make this duality work to create a new form of English writing.

People in Alvarez's Fiction. Alvarez's most vividly drawn characters are the fictional García sisters, who are based closely upon her own family, and the Mirabal sisters, who are historical figures fictionalized from available historical fragments and oral histories. Less fully realized are her male characters, who are often, but not always, portrayed as opposing forces, ranging from the merely paternalistic Papí to the conflicted but sadistic captain, Peña, and the villainous dictator, Trujillo.

LONG FICTION

1991   How the García Girls Lost Their Accents
1994   In the Time of the Butterflies
1997   ¡Yo!
2000   In the Name of Salomé

POETRY

1984   Homecoming: Poems
1995   The Other Side: El Otro Lado
1996   Homecoming: New and Collected Poems
1998   Seven Trees

NONFICTION

1998   Something to Declare

CHILDREN'S LITERATURE

2000   The Secret Footprints

EDITED TEXTS

1979   Old Age Ain't for Sissies (with Pamolu Oldham)

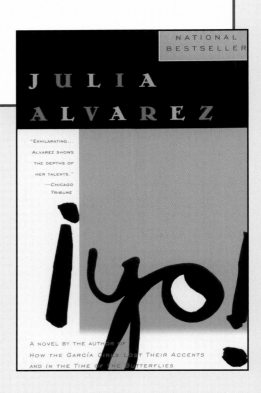

BIBLIOGRAPHY

Bing, Jonathan. "Julia Alvarez: Books That Cross Borders." *Publishers Weekly* 243, no. 51 (December 16, 1996): 38–39.

"Julia Alvarez: Dominican-American Novelist and Poet." In *Latino Biographies*. Paramus, N.J.: Globe Fearon, 1994.

Lyons, Bonnie, and Bill Oliver. "A Clean Windshield: An Interview with Julia Alvarez." In *Passion and Craft: Conversations with Notable Writers*. Urbana: University of Illinois Press, 1998.

Morales, Ed. "Madam Butterfly: How Julia Alvarez Found Her Accent." *Village Voice Literary Supplement*, November 13, 1994, p.13.

Ortiz-Marquez, Maribel. "From Third World Politics to First World Practices: Contemporary Latina Writers in the United States." In *Interventions: Feminist Dialogues on Third World Women's Literature and Film*, edited by Ghosh Bishnupriya and Bose Brinda. New York: Garland, 1997.

Rosario-Sievert, Heather. "Anxiety, Repression, and Return: The Language of Julia Alvarez." *Readerly/Writerly Texts: Essays on Literature, Literary/Textual Criticism, and Pedagogy* 4, no. 2 (Spring/Summer 1997).

———. "Conversation with Julia Alvarez." *Review: Latin American Literature and Arts* 54 (Spring 1997): 31–37.

Vela, Richard. "Daughter of Invention: The Poetry of Julia Alvarez." *Postscript: Publication of the Philological Association of the Carolinas* 16 (1999).

HOW THE GARCÍA GIRLS LOST THEIR ACCENTS

Genre: Novel
Subgenre: Bicultural/immigrant fiction
Published: New York, 1991
Time period: 1960s to the 1980s
Setting: United States

Themes and Issues. The challenge facing immigrants to the United States is how to fit in yet still retain their identities. If this balancing act is easier in some ways for children, their adaptation challenges the family dynamic when their newly adopted cultural traditions and customs conflict with those of their parents. Yolanda García feels the loss of her first language as deeply as a hole in her heart when it is replaced by the acquired language of her new homeland.

The Plot. Yolanda García, a writer, has returned to the Dominican Republic to visit her cousins, who were left behind twenty-nine years earlier when the family fled Trujillo's regime. She goes off to find and eat guavas, bringing the country back into her body. The novel moves backward through time from the first chapter's setting of 1989 to the final chapter's 1956.

The narrative reveals the history of the García family from their present careers, marriages, love affairs, and family relationships to earlier successes and failures, education, experimentation, and the changing political, social, and cultural worlds of both the United States and the Dominican Republic. Several chapters focus on Yolanda and all involve her in some way. The final chapter again focuses on Yolanda, the teller of these stories, both as a little girl and as a mature writer. It locates the themes of the book firmly in the body—the body political, the body sexual, the body physical, the body violated.

Analysis. The voices in the fifteen chapters of this novel knit together the worlds of the García girls. The story begins in their adult middle age, after they have spent twenty-nine years in the United States, and moves backward in time to show their assimilation into North American culture through the lens of present successes and sorrows. Fleeing a dangerous paradise, the García family immigrates to the fallen world of a New York City full of promise and pain. In each chapter, stories reveal their losses, of their accents as well as the lore and culture of their homeland. Conflicts arise between the two cultures and between the attitudes and values of the parents and those that the four girls acquire in the United States.

The key to understanding the stories is literally the concluding image of the novel, an

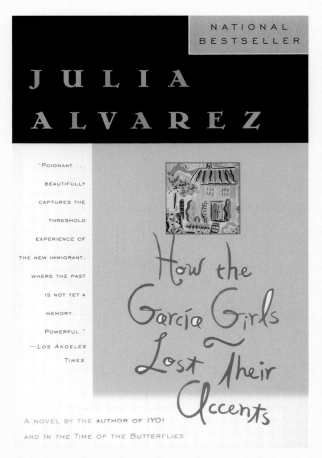

How the Garcia Girls Lost Their Accents announced the arrival of an important new Latino voice in American fiction.

In the Time of the Butterflies fictionally re-creates the day-to-day struggles and tragic loss of the real-life Mirabal sisters. Pictured from left to right are Maria, Minerva, and Patria Mirabal, all of whom lost their lives under the Trujillo regime in the Dominican Republic.

image of a nightmare in which an abused cat wails "over some violation that lies at the center of my art." As seems to be true of all of Alvarez's fiction, the telling and retelling of the stories of the individuals and the community create the life of those characters and their communities. However, to tell those stories the writer must violate the privacy and often the trust of their subjects, a theme to which Alvarez returns in her novel *¡Yo!*.

SOURCES FOR FURTHER STUDY

Barak, Julie. "'Turning and Turning in the Widening Gyre': A Second Coming into Language in Julia Alvarez's *How the García Girls Lost Their Accents*." *Melus: The Journal of the Society for the Study of the Multi-Ethnic Literature of the United States* 23, no. 1 (Spring 1998): 159–176.

Hoffman, Joan M. "'She Wants to Be Called Yolanda Now': Identity, Language, and the Third Sister in *How the García Girls Lost Their Accents*." *Bilingual Review/La Revista Bilinque* 23, no. 1 (January–April 1998): 21–27.

Huddle, David. "Ordering the Family Confusion: An Essay on Julia Alvarez's 'The Kiss.'" In *About These Stories: Fiction for Fiction Writers and Readers*. Edited by David Huddle, Gita Orth, and Allen Shepherd. New York: McGraw-Hill, 1994.

Luis, William. "A Search for Identity in Julia Alvarez's *How the García Girls Lost Their Accents*." In *Dance Between Two Cultures: Latino Caribbean Literature Written in the United States*. Nashville, Tenn.: Vanderbilt University Press, 1997.

IN THE TIME OF THE BUTTERFLIES
Genre: Novel
Subgenre: Historical fiction
Published: New York, 1994
Time period: From 1924 to 1960
Setting: Dominican Republic

Themes and Issues. The courage to resist a dictator is a rare quality; the sacrifices made by these ordinary women serve to inspire the struggle against all despotism. Historical figures, the Mirabal sisters are fictionally re-created in this novel to provide a deeper truth about their lives than either biography or hagiography.

The Plot. The surviving sister, Dedé, tells the story of the four Mirabal sisters, three of whom were murdered on November 25, 1960, by agents of the regime of Rafael Leónidas Trujillo Molina, dictator of the Dominican Republic. The plot of *In the Time of the Butterflies* portrays the struggles of the Mirabal family and, by extension, the rest of Dominican society, to create and maintain the normal life activities of family and community in the face of the increasing outrages committed by Trujillo and members of his regime.

Born into a large extended family, the Mirabal sisters go to a convent school, form friendships, are immersed in their religion, form ambitions to enter the university, have careers, fall in love, marry, and raise families. As their knowledge of Trujillo's evil regime grows, so does their resistance to it. They become forcefully involved in the underground when it becomes more apparent that every citizen will need to take arms against the dictator. Trujillo and his henchmen fight back by intimidating the populace, arresting entire families and torturing, raping, and murdering them.

Despite the increasing danger, Minerva speaks out against Trujillo, and finally all of the Mirabal sisters and their families become active in the underground opposition to the dictator. An important subplot concerns the infidelity of Dominican men and the subordinate sexual, social, and economic position of women in Dominican society. A related subplot involves the Mirabal sisters' discovery and acknowledgment of their half-sisters and thus sisterhood figuratively as well as literally.

Analysis. Alvarez's novel reveals the "special courage" that inspired the Mirabals to risk their lives to overthrow Trujillo. Alvarez considered a historical fiction the best way to "travel through the human heart" to create the Mirabals of her imagination. Her characters are neither the "real" women of fact nor the mythic women of popular legend but, as created fictional characters, they are true to the spirit of liberty. Based on the oral traditions she collected about the resistance, Alvarez creates a portrait of *las Mirraposas*, the

Dominican people's code name for the four Mirabal sisters. Three were murdered on November 25, 1960; one, Dedé, survived and thus must tell the story of her sisters and the others who died to free their country.

Dedé's remembrances of her family and the terror of the secret police gives this novel its elegiac yet celebratory tone. Like the Dominican Republic itself, Dedé can now look forward to a future of healing and progress. At the end of the novel she sits with Lío, another of the former revolutionaries, both now in their early seventies, observing the signs of prosperity and material progress and wondering, "Was it for this, the sacrifice of the butterflies, these fragile, beautiful women?" The real progress, she decides, is that the young people are not haunted by fear and hate and can claim their own country.

Butterflies symbolize the beauty of the Mirabal sisters and the fragility of life. *Sol y Mariposas* (*Sun and Butterflies*) by Alfredo Arreguin, oil on canvas, 1998.

The novel is built around three sections, in each of which a sister reveals, in her own narrative voice, her actions, thoughts, fears, and loves. The Mirabals' awareness of the evil and dangers of the Trujillo regime emerges with whispered stories of murdered families and sexual predation. The structure thus develops a set of tensions that informs and reveals the themes—and the emotional costs to the Mirabals as their lives proceed on two levels, one of love, marriage, and family and another of growing involvement in the political work of the underground.

The tension deepens as the "butterflies" are imprisoned under brutal conditions, tortured, and abused. However, the imprisoned sisters' strength grows so that even their release and their restoration to a "normal" life does not lessen their activity or their importance to the underground. The personal and political themes come together when the women are ambushed on the last of their once-a-month visits to their men who remain imprisoned in a remote location in the mountains. The sisters' martyrdom raises them to the status of folk heroes.

SOURCES FOR FURTHER STUDY

Brown, Isabel Zakrzewski. "Historiographic Metafiction in *In the Time of the Butterflies*." *South Atlantic Review* 64, no. 2 (Spring, 1999).

Martinez, Elizabeth Coonrod. "Recovering a Space for a History Between Imperialism and Patriarchy: Julia Alvarez's *In the Time of the Butterflies*." *Thamyris: Mythmaking from Past to Present* 5, no. 2 (Autumn, 1998): 263–279.

¡YO!

Genre: Novel
Subgenre: Metafiction
Published: 1997
Time period: 1980s
Setting: United States; Dominican Republic

Themes and Issues. Two principal themes structure this novel. The first is the theme of art mirroring life and the nature and function of stories in human life. The second is the search for love. Other themes appear as well, such as the nature of family, the conflict between career and family, and the appropriation of the female writer by her readers.

The Plot. Yolanda García's first novel has sold well and earned good reviews—from everyone but her family, who feels exposed and misrepresented by it. Despite Yolanda's arguments that "art mirrors life" and "one writes what one knows," family members, friends, and acquaintances step forward to tell their side of the story and offer their take on the beautiful, tormented, talented immigrant writer who desperately wants her destiny to be a writer not to interfere with her powerful need to love and be loved. Yolanda's wedding (her third) at the novel's end brings together most of the characters.

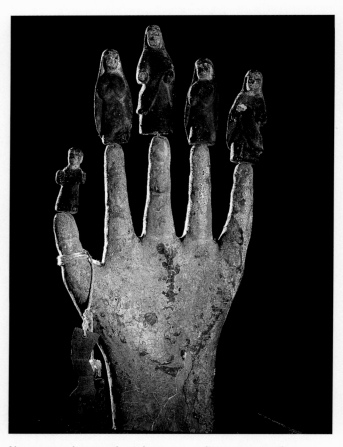

Alvarez uses her creative talents as a writer to oppose the heavy hand of dictatorship and to express the importance of truth. The oppression experienced at the hands of a powerful dictatorship is echoed in *La Mano Poderosa* (*The Powerful Hand*) by an unknown Puerto Rican artist, ca. 1875–1925.

Yolanda's wedding, as well as her father's decision to bless and love his daughter, offer a healing and unifying ending to the novel with the promise that both love and art will triumph.

Analysis. Alvarez analyzes the relationship between art and life. Her argument is both political and psychological in its exploration of the role that repression plays in stimulating and stifling art as well as the role of art in liberating both individual and state from repression. Yolanda García resists the heavy hand of state dictatorship, parental brutality, and spousal abuse. That one must be free to live and create, to tell one's story, is the credo of this book. The lie must be exposed whatever its cause, whatever the consequences. Even Yolanda herself is held to this challenge. As a teacher of writing she has apparently appropriated a student's story. As a student she has abused the friendship of a beloved and loving professor. As a child, as a sister, as a friend, she has betrayed confidences, exposed weaknesses, and entered into irresponsible relationships.

Yolanda is not a saint but a human being; she has come back to tell her story, warts and all. Thus, the novel emphasizes that the story permits catharsis, engaging the reader through the psychological processes of pity and fear and helping the reader to live as fully as possible.

Alvarez suggests that repression of the natural and human impulse to shape one's reality by telling one's story is despotic and destructive. Storytelling, she argues, lets in the light; it is organic, life-giving, healing, and affirming. "Tell them of our journey," Yolanda's father instructs her at the end of the novel. Like the biblical Lazarus, the writer is to "come back, come back to tell you all." Such instruction can be profoundly disturbing, yet inspiring. This hopeful and optimistic theme emerges most clearly in the wedding of Yolanda and a Kansas farm boy.

Splendidly chaotic, its pastoralism is optimistic and healing. In the chapter entitled "The Wedding Guests," each of the guests articulates his or her principal "issues" with Yolanda as the narrative point of view shifts from one to the next. In doing so, each frees Yolanda from the prison of the past just as Doug, her third husband, frees the ewe from its entrapping wire so that it may rejoin the flock. Such scenes demonstrate Alvarez's ability to weave scene, image, symbolic action, plot, and character together into a subtle and satisfying whole that articulates a profound belief in the positive function of art and the ultimate importance of the storyteller to humanity. The novel is a superbly crafted and satisfying artistic achievement and an uplifting, unsentimental, and honest examination of what it means to be a human immigrant, woman, artist, writer, lover, student, stepmother, daughter, friend, cousin.

Other Works

HOMECOMING: NEW AND COLLECTED POEMS (1996). Alvarez originally published a volume titled *Homecoming: Poems* in 1984, and she reissued it in 1996 with new poems added. These poems demonstrate an impressive command over nuanced expression, subtle sound patterning, a keen eye for the extraordinary power of the ordinary, and a strong narrative that carries the reader forward. Especially successful are the "Housekeeping" poems and "33," a sonnet sequence with additional sonnets added for this edition. The additional sonnets convey a strong political tone absent in the original edition. Many of the "Housekeeping" poems reveal fundamental principles of human conduct. In "Making Our Beds," for example, Mother's insistence that the corners be made just so into the "hospital corner" and her stories about her wedding bed suggest, in their images and in their silences, a world of expectations and appropriate behaviors. The duties of child, wife, and mother are all enacted in this detailed poem about the family's beds.

The poems in the "Heroines" section celebrate a variety of heroines. "Against Cinderella" is perhaps one of the most witty, ending by asserting "That some of us have learned to go barefoot knowing the mate to one foot is the other" and suggesting the need for self-knowledge and independence. The "Redwing Sonnets" demonstrate Alvarez's agility with the form of the sonnet sequence. They contain a strong narrative line, employ the traditional and unifying theme of the poet's song, and have the sound of good conversation.

THE OTHER SIDE: EL OTRO LADO (1995). This collection of poems is divided into five sections introduced by "Bilingual Sestina" as the first section, which argues the power and worth of bilingualism: that one language cannot say all that matters to the poet's heart. The next section, "The Gladys Poems," celebrates the woman who served Alvarez's family as pantry maid but who was also friend, tutor, confidant, singer of songs, and teller of stories. The third section, "Making Up the Past," tells of the family's fleeing the Dominican Republic for a new life in New York City. As immigrants, the newcomers are lost in an utterly foreign urban world that is at the same time exciting and promising. The narrator describes learning about her world, her body, and her new chosen language as "nothing left to cry for, nothing left but the story of our family's grand adventure from one language to another." The poet's antidote for such losses is clearly to make stories that both express the loss and create hope.

In the fourth section, "The Joe Poems," are found a number of fine poems about language; one of the best and most moving is "Touchstone." The poet calls her lover from New York City's La Guardia Airport just before getting on a plane, in a panic because she may die in a plane crash but also because she has lost a

Sisterhood and female independence, common themes in Alvarez's work, are reflected in *Five Girls from Quaratingueta* by an unknown artist.

word, the word for the stone that tells whether something is genuine. When her lover responds "touchstone," the idea and the image are then elaborated to become the test of love as well as of language.

Alvarez's award-winning poem "Bookmaking" is the fourth poem in this section. The powerful imagery of several poems in this section, such as "the werewolf paw" in "Staying Up Alone," are reminiscent of those of the metaphysical seventeenth-century English poet John Donne. The final section, "The Other Side: *El Otro Lado*," successfully blends a strong story line with impressive control of language and image and sound to articulate the poet's awareness that she cannot return to live in her homeland, that she has crossed "the watery darkness to the shore I've made up on the other side."

SOMETHING TO DECLARE (1998). Generated by questions from her readers, these essays address many of the same themes as Alvarez's novels, stories, and poems but do so, as she says, by giving a straight answer. Her concerns focus on the condition of the bilingual writer, the nature of language and family, and her relationship with her parents and with her two "native countries": the United States, where she was born and has lived and worked her adult life, and the Dominican Republic, her childhood home and the home of her heart.

In "La Gringuita," subtitled "On Losing a Native Language," Alvarez comments at length on the irony of her speaking her "native" language, Spanish, with an American English accent. She speaks her childhood Spanish perfectly but feels more at home discussing adult themes, topics, and emotions in English because her formal training in the language of adult discourse was in English.

Other essays deal with the timeless themes of growing up. She discusses her relationship with her beloved father, who, although a successful medical doctor, was never comfortable speaking in English. She also discusses her relationship with her mother, whose English had been honed in a Boston boarding school in the 1940s. Alvarez explores her close relationships with her three sisters in various contexts, including how they felt about the stan-dards of physical beauty enacted in the Miss America contests in the era before the country's multiethnicity was recognized and celebrated. "Picky Eater" details how cultural values are revealed in food customs and behaviors that turn mealtimes into sites of struggle against performance pressures. The themes of loss, of choices made and others cut off, of aging, and of marital harmonies and dissonances all variously appear in these essays.

In her 1998 collection of essays, *Something to Declare*, Alvarez emphasized the importance of knowing "the secret heart of each other's lives." She stresses that storytelling, captured in this scene of Manhattan's Lower East Side by Kindred McLeary, creates community and decreases an individual's isolation.

Resources

Of Alvarez's manuscripts, only the original papers from the sonnet sequence "33" have a home; the New York Public Library acquired those manuscripts. The rest remain in Alvarez's possession.

Alta Gracia Foundation. Julia Alvarez and her husband, Bill Eichner, established a foundation, Alta Gracia, the first objective of which was to become a sustainable organic coffee farm to enable the foundation to become self-supporting. The second goal was to develop a literacy center for Dominicans, widening eventually to include an arts center that would integrate people from both the Dominican Republic and other countries.

Voices from the Gaps: Women Writers of Color. An Internet research project devoted to the works of nonwhite female American writers features a page on Julia Alvarez, with a biography, a selected bibliography, criticisms, and related links. (http://voices.cla.umn.edu/authors/Julia Alvarez.html)

Postcolonial Studies at Emory. This excellent academic site, created by Susan Walker at Emory University, has many links to substantial academic sites dealing with postcolonial literature, theorists, terms, and issues. Its page devoted to Julia Alvarez features a biography, a discussion of major themes in her works, and lists of books by and about Alvarez. (http://www.emory.edu/ENGLISH/Bahri/Alvarez.html)

The Politics of Fiction. The on-line magazine *Frontera* features an interview with Alvarez by Marny Requa that appeared in 1997. (http://www.fronteramag.com/issue5/Alvarez/)

On Tour: Julia Alvarez. The Bookwire Web site hosts an interview with Alvarez that originally appeared in the *Hungry Mind Review: An Independent Book Review* in 1995, when she was touring the country to promote *The Other Side: El Otro Lado.* (http://www.bookwire.com/hmr/Review/talvarez.html)

THEODORE C. HUMPHREY

Sherwood Anderson

BORN: September 13, 1876, Camden, Ohio
DIED: March 8, 1941, Colón, Panama Canal Zone
IDENTIFICATION: Early twentieth-century writer of novels, short fiction, poetry, plays, and nonfiction; best known for his stories of life in the midwestern United States, especially *Winesburg, Ohio*.

Sherwood Anderson wrote about American life with a psychological insight and a concern for social issues that earned him awards and international recognition. He was noted for his innovative style, which combined common speech with emotional experience, and he influenced many writers who followed him, most notably William Faulkner and Ernest Hemingway. Anderson's *Winesburg, Ohio* (1919) remains a classic taught in high schools and colleges. An episodic novel, it shows a young man growing up in an Ohio town, as well as the unusual inner lives of the town's residents. Other works, such as his novel *Poor White* (1920) and his short story "The Egg" (1921) continue to receive critical attention.

The Writer's Life

Sherwood Anderson was born on September 13, 1876, in Camden, Ohio, the third of six children. His mother, Emma, a strong woman, was beaten down by self-sacrifice. His father, Irwin, was a romantic storyteller but a poor provider for his family, due partly to his nature and partly to the increasing obsolescence of his skills as a harness maker.

Anderson's childhood struggles to make ends meet earned him the nickname "Jobby" around the time this photograph was taken. The exact date of the photograph is unknown.

Growing Up. During Anderson's first eight years, his family moved from town to town in Ohio, finally settling in Clyde, on which he based his fictional town of Winesburg. In his memoirs, he views Clyde with nostalgia. Yet, in his fiction, he reveals the small town's dark side: a lack of opportunity and a sometimes oppressive morality. Anderson worked from an early age, earning the nickname "Jobby." Although his school attendance was brief and often interrupted, he read a great deal, including books by Mark Twain and James Fenimore Cooper. A year after his mother died of tuberculosis in 1895, Anderson moved to Chicago, Illinois, where he worked as a stock boy in a warehouse.

Anderson's life in Chicago was difficult, and he almost welcomed the change and excitement of the Spanish-American War of 1898. After he joined the Army, he was sent to Cuba in January 1899, nearly six months after Spain surrendered. Upon his return, he attended Wittenberg Academy, a prep school. He spent only a year there, but it was a pleasant and active year, full of intellectual stimulation both in class and at the Oaks, the boardinghouse where he stayed.

Becoming a Businessman. An older boarder at the Oaks offered Anderson a job in Chicago, and Anderson became a successful businessman, writing and selling advertising copy. He also wrote articles and columns, first for a trade magazine, *Agricultural*

YOUR COUNTRY CALLS YOU

R·M·WRIGH '98.

Anderson answered the call of the U.S. Army, reflected in this 1898 recruitment poster, when he enrolled to serve in the Spanish-American War. The Army provided Anderson with a quick escape from his life as a laborer in Chicago.

Advertising. In 1904 he married the first of four wives, Cornelia Lane. She came from a respectable middle-class family, and, to Anderson, she represented social and economic success. The couple moved to Cleveland and then Elyria, Ohio, where Anderson ran a business selling roof cement and paint. The Andersons had three children: Robert Lane in 1907, John Sherwood in 1908, and Marion in 1911. Anderson and his wife were a popular couple, and Anderson appeared to be the perfect businessman.

A Breaking Point. However, on November 28, 1912, Anderson abruptly left his business to move to Chicago and become an artist. By 1912 his outlook had been changing for over two years, during which time he became a socialist, wrote fiction late at night, and neglected his business. He did walk out of his office one day, but his move was less a rebellious decision than a nervous breakdown. Still, for Anderson, becoming a writer instead of a businessman was both a moral choice and the only way he could be truly happy.

HIGHLIGHTS IN ANDERSON'S LIFE

1876 Sherwood Anderson is born on September 13, in Camden, Ohio.

1884 Family settles in Clyde, Ohio, the inspiration for Anderson's fictional Winesburg.

1895 Mother, Emma Anderson, dies.

1896 Anderson moves from Clyde to Chicago, working as a laborer.

1898 Enters U.S. Army.

1899 Enrolls in Wittenberg Academy.

1900 Moves back to Chicago, working as advertising salesman and copywriter; begins writing poems and fiction.

1904 Marries Cornelia Lane.

1906 Becomes president of United Factories Company in Cleveland, Ohio.

1907 Son Robert is born; Anderson manages business in Elyria, Ohio; writes poetry and fiction.

1908 Son John is born.

1911 Daughter Marion is born

1912 Anderson suffers nervous breakdown; leaves work in Elyria for life in Chicago.

1913 Works as advertising copywriter; becomes part of artistic "Chicago Renaissance."

1916 Publishes first novel, *Windy McPherson's Son;* divorces wife and marries Tennessee Mitchell.

1918 Publishes book of poetry *Mid-American Chants.*

1919 Publishes *Winesburg, Ohio,* his most successful and best-known book.

1920 Publishes novel *Poor White.*

1921 Publishes *The Triumph of the Egg,* a book of poetry and short fiction; wins Dial award.

1923 Ends marriage to Tennessee Mitchell.

1924 Publishes *A Story Teller's Story;* marries third wife, Elizabeth Prall.

1926 Goes on lecture tour; publishes semi-autobiographical *Tar: A Midwest Childhood* and nonfiction *Sherwood Anderson's Notebook.*

1927 Buys two local newspapers in Marion, Virginia, running them for two years.

1929 Divorces Elizabeth Prall.

1930 Becomes active supporter of workers' issues, a theme in later fiction.

1933 Publishes *Death in the Woods and Other Stories;* marries Eleanor Copenhaver.

1934 Produces stage version of *Winesburg, Ohio.*

1937 Publishes book of plays, including *Winesburg, Ohio;* is elected to National Institute of Arts and Letters.

1941 Dies of peritonitis in the Panama Canal Zone on March 8, while touring South America.

1942 *Sherwood Anderson's Memoirs* is published posthumously.

When Anderson moved to Chicago, he worked again as an advertising copywriter, but he was now more dedicated to art than ever. His wife and children moved with him, but in mid-1914 he broke that tie also, and Cornelia moved to Indiana. Meanwhile, Anderson established himself as a writer and a member of the "Chicago Renaissance," along with Ben Hecht, Carl Sandburg, and others. Conversations with fellow writers introduced him to the theories of Sigmund Freud; the writings of William Dean Howells, Gertrude Stein, and James Joyce; and arguments for pacifism and anarchism, as well as socialism.

Anderson published his poetry in literary magazines, such as the *Little Review*, *Poetry*, and *Seven Arts*. In 1916 he published *Windy McPherson's Son*, and in 1917 he published *Marching Men*. Both were somewhat autobiographical novels that Anderson had written in Elyria. They were followed in 1918 by *Mid-American Chants*, a book of poetry.

The Mature Writer. The years 1917 to 1921 were the best of Anderson's writing career. His most famous book, *Winesburg, Ohio*, was published in 1919—a strange and tender novel that was daring in style and impressive in psychological insight. *The Triumph of the Egg: A Book of Impressions from American Life in Tales and Poems* (1921) and *Horses and Men: Tales Long and Short* (1923) contain some of Anderson's best short stories. *Poor White*, published in 1920, was less famous than *Winesburg, Ohio* but is sometimes considered Anderson's best novel, especially in its depiction of the damage of industrialization to a midwestern town. In 1921, Anderson won an award from *Dial* magazine, the first such award it issued.

In 1916 Anderson married Tennessee Mitchell, an aspiring sculptor who shared his commitment to art. Anderson and Mitchell had a "modern" marriage, each leading separate lives, often keeping separate residences. Early in 1921 the couple was invited to visit Paris and London, where Anderson met the writers Gertrude Stein, James Joyce, and Ford Madox Ford, as well as the poet laureate John Masefield. Anderson drew praise in the early 1920s from such noted American writers as F. Scott Fitzgerald, Ernest Hemingway, and Sinclair Lewis. The Andersons' marriage fell apart after 1921; they divorced in 1923. In 1924 Anderson married his third wife, Elizabeth Prall.

Anderson's writing during this time was strong but uneven. *Many Marriages*, a semi-successful novel published in 1923, concerns a businessman who abandons his wife and children to run off with his secretary. Anderson also wrote a number of memoirs in these years, such as *A Story Teller's Story* (1924). Public image was vital to Anderson, and he crafted his carefully, although not always truthfully, in his writing and in his persona.

Loss of Reputation, Rural Retirement. By the mid-1920s, Anderson was past his peak as a writer, and critical opinion of his work turned harsh. Ernest Hemingway's *The Torrents of Spring* (1926) parodies Anderson's novel *Dark Laughter* (1925). Anderson himself seemed to realize his artistic inspiration was ebbing, and in 1927 he became a country gentleman, purchasing and editing two local newspapers—one Republican and one Democratic—in Marion, Virginia. He wrote weekly columns, published as *Hello Towns!* in 1929. That same year, Anderson and his third wife, Elizabeth, divorced, and he returned to Chicago.

Final Years. From late 1929 to his death in 1941, Anderson remade himself yet again, under the influence of Eleanor Copenhaver. Anderson had met Eleanor in Marion, and she accompanied him to Chicago, where they married in 1933. Anderson's new wife was socially conscious, and she influenced his life and work. He supported the strikers in Danville, Indiana, and examined the effects of industrialism on workers in both his nonfiction, such as *Perhaps Women* (1931), and his fiction, such as *Kit Brandon* (1936). He continued to write essays, which he collected in *No Swank* (1934), *Puzzled America* (1935), and *Home Town* (1940). In his later years, Anderson rewrote some of his works as plays, including *Winesburg, Ohio*.

The Writer's Work

Although he is known primarily for his novel *Winesburg, Ohio*, Sherwood Anderson also wrote short fiction, poetry, nonfiction, and plays. His work is uneven, and even his advocates consider some of his novels to be "palpably bad efforts," badly structured or flawed in style. Critics differ in their opinions of Anderson's worst novel, but they agree that his best work includes not only *Winesburg, Ohio* but also his novel *Poor White*, his memoir *A Story Teller's Story*, and a number of short stories. Anderson's plays are dramatic versions of *Winesburg, Ohio* and some of his short stories.

Themes in Anderson's Fiction. While Anderson grew and changed as a person and a writer, his central concerns remained remarkably stable. The most consistent theme in his work is a strong autobiographical slant. Ironically, his memoirs themselves are not factually reliable and seem to be concerned less with truth than with mythmaking about himself and those around him. However, his fiction often offers deep insight into his life and character. Repeatedly, Anderson returns to three main aspects of his growing up: his mother, his father, and his own coming-of-age.

Anderson's youthful feelings about his father may be seen in *Windy McPherson's Son*. Windy McPherson is depicted as a boasting fool who disgraces his family and contributes to the early death of his overworked wife. Later, Anderson grew more sympathetic toward his father's failures, seeing them as the fault of society. This viewpoint is reflected in Anderson's treatment of failures in *Winesburg, Ohio* and "The Egg" in *The Triumph of the Egg*. Anderson's presentation of his father in his memoirs is mixed. He admires his father's romantic, storytelling streak but condemns his failure to fulfill family responsibilities. Anderson's portrayal of his mother is both more consistent and more sympathetic. In his memoirs, he shows her as mysterious but quietly courageous. His fiction, including *Winesburg, Ohio*, *Windy McPherson's Son*, and *Dark Laughter*, is full of kind women worn down by society, and especially by marriage. Many of Anderson's works also concern the coming-of-age of a confused but admirable young man, sometimes creative, sometimes energetic in business, and sometimes turning from the world of work and money to the world of beauty and art.

Anderson also used events from his adult life in his work. For instance, the hero of *Many Marriages* leaves a stifling job, along with his wife and child, which echoes Anderson's 1912 break with business to become an artist in Chicago. *Kit Brandon* draws on Anderson's experiences in Virginia, including the knowledge of southern culture that he gained as owner and editor of two small-town newspapers. "The Man's Story," in *Horses and Men*, depicts Anderson's first stay in Chicago and his difficult, dreary life there.

A second theme in Anderson's fiction is that of communication, love, and sexuality and the social obstacles facing them. Influenced by writers as varied as Sigmund Freud and Walt Whitman, Anderson repeatedly created characters stifled by frustration and loneliness and turned into grotesques, as in *Winesburg, Ohio*. Some of his characters reach a kind of freedom and rebirth, usually by leaving comfortable yet confining marriages or jobs. Anderson's earlier work is usually set in small towns, which his heroes usually leave—as Anderson did—when they find their true selves. In his later work, such as *Beyond Desire* (1932), he champions the working man, oppressed by industrialization, and his heroes become social reformers—as Anderson himself eventually did.

A third theme of Anderson's work is less psychological and more social. He consistently and accurately captured the atmosphere and social structure of his settings—a small Ohio

These three photographs reveal the ever-changing persona of Sherwood Anderson. Anderson, who had a knack for reinventing himself, posed in coat and hat for the *Chicago Daily News* in April of 1922 (left). The dates of the above photographs, both part of a collection at the Newberry Library in Chicago, are unknown.

town, the rural South, or a city, such as Chicago. He also showed the effects of the social changes he had seen in his lifetime, especially the industrialization of the Midwest.

Anderson's Style. Despite his clear influences and his acknowledged influence on others, Anderson is unique as a stylist. In fact, while writers both praise his innovation and criticize the unevenness of his work, they too rarely see the interrelation of these two qualities. Anderson had a clear and unusual personal vision, and he was willing to take chances to realize it in prose. *Winesburg, Ohio* contains the best of Anderson's emotional, impressionistic writing, which always suggests more than it actually says.

Anderson experimented with the novelistic form and, more successfully, with that of the short story. While Anderson generally had difficulty plotting a unified novel, some of his

NONFICTION

1924   A Story Teller's Story
1925   The Modern Writer
1926   Tar: A Midwest Childhood
1926   Sherwood Anderson's Notebook
1929   Hello Towns!
1931   Perhaps Women
1934   No Swank
1935   Puzzled America
1940   Home Town
1942   Sherwood Anderson's Memoirs
1953   The Letters of Sherwood Anderson
1984   Sherwood Anderson: Selected Letters
1985   Letters to Bab: Sherwood Anderson to Marietta D. Finley, 1916–1933

LONG FICTION

1916   Windy McPherson's Son
1917   Marching Men
1919   Winesburg, Ohio
1920   Poor White
1923   Many Marriages
1925   Dark Laughter
1932   Beyond Desire
1936   Kit Brandon

SHORT FICTION

1921   The Triumph of the Egg: A Book of Impressions from American Life in Tales and Poems
1923   Horses and Men: Tales Long and Short
1933   Death in the Woods and Other Stories

PLAYS

1937   Plays: Winesburg, Ohio, and Others

POETRY

1918   Mid-American Chants
1927   A New Testament

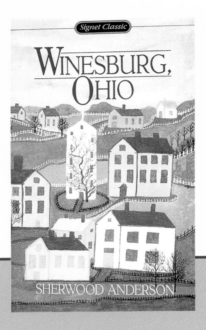

books successfully utilize that weakness, such as *Kit Brandon*, in which dual narrators tell the same story, or *Winesburg, Ohio*, in which fragmentary stories convey the isolated, fragmentary lives of the book's characters. Still, Anderson's shorter works are clearly more successful in terms of both structure and prose style. He despised trick endings, as in the stories of O. Henry, and argued that the essence of the short story is in its characters.

BIBLIOGRAPHY

Anderson, David D. *Sherwood Anderson: An Introduction and Interpretation*. New York: Holt, 1967.

———, ed. *Critical Essays on Sherwood Anderson*. Boston: G. K. Hall, 1981.

Burbank, Rex. *Sherwood Anderson*. New York: Twayne Publishers, 1964.

Howe, Irving. *Sherwood Anderson*. New York: William Sloane Associates, 1951. Reprint. Stanford, Calif.: Stanford University Press, 1966.

Papinchak, Robert Allen. *Sherwood Anderson: A Study of the Short Fiction*. New York: Twayne Publishers, 1992.

Schevill, James. *Sherwood Anderson: His Life and Work*. Denver, Colo.: University of Denver Press, 1951.

Small, Judy Jo. *A Reader's Guide to the Short Stories of Sherwood Anderson*. Boston: G. K. Hall, 1994.

Sutton, William A. *The Road to Winesburg: A Mosaic of the Imaginative Life of Sherwood Anderson*. Metuchen, N.J.: Scarecrow Press, 1972.

Weber, Brom. *Sherwood Anderson*. Minneapolis: University of Minnesota Press, 1964.

White, Ray Lewis, ed. *The Achievement of Sherwood Anderson*. Chapel Hill: University of North Carolina Press, 1966.

Reader's Guide to Major Works

POOR WHITE

Genre: Novel
Subgenre: *Bildungsroman*, social critique
Published: New York, 1920
Time period: Late nineteenth century
Setting: Mississippi; Bidwell, Ohio

Themes and Issues. Sherwood Anderson explores some of the concerns of the earlier *Winesburg, Ohio* in this more unified and socially conscious book. Hugh McVey begins as an innocent and advances financially when he invents labor-saving machines, but he finally realizes that industrialization is bad for his town. His marriage to Clara Butterworth helps him mature, both morally and physically. Anderson critically explores the effects of industrialization on a small Ohio town, representing in Bidwell his own midwestern experience.

The Plot. Hugh McVey is the main character, beginning as a "poor white" boy in Mississippi. An innocent, he physically resembles young Abraham Lincoln, whom Anderson admired. Clearly influenced by Mark Twain, Anderson makes his protagonist the son of a lazy, directionless man who lives on the river. Hugh himself is content to drift through life until he begins work at a railway station in Mudcat Landing, Mississippi, when he is fourteen. There he is befriended by the manager, Henry Shephard, and his wife, Sarah, a practical and hard-working northerner. Under the Shephards'

SOME INSPIRATIONS BEHIND ANDERSON'S WORK

As a child, Anderson loved romantic reading: James Fenimore Cooper, Sir Walter Scott, Jules Verne, and the popular idealized biographies of Abraham Lincoln, Napoleon Bonaparte, and Jesse James. Such books appealed to a young man's need for excitement, but most of them also instilled a sense of morality and of the need to find purpose in life. Two other early influences were Mark Twain and Harriet Beecher Stowe, in whom Anderson saw critical examination of the follies and vices of society.

The author's views on sexuality—its holiness and healing ability, and the dangers of its repression—came mainly from D. H. Lawrence, Walt Whitman, and Sigmund Freud. These authors' writings encouraged Anderson to tackle questions of sex and marriage frankly in his own work. Theodore Dreiser's novel *Sister Carrie*, republished in 1911 after being suppressed for eleven years, also influenced Anderson in this area.

Stylistically, Anderson was an experimentalist. Critics have noted many influences in his later prose: from avant-garde writer Gertrude Stein's *Tender Buttons: Objects, Food, Rooms* (1914) to James Joyce's stream-of-consciousness style. However, Anderson's writing also shows the influence of Mark Twain, William Dean Howells, and others. The structure—or lack of structure—of *Winesburg, Ohio* may have been influenced by Edgar Lee Masters's *Spoon River Anthology* (1915), a series of poems depicting the interwoven lives of those lying in a cemetery in a small town.

John Warner Norton's oil-on-canvas painting *Light and Shadow* (The Art Institute of Chicago), painted around 1924, reflects the encroachment of the industrial world on an agrarian lifestyle, a subject addressed in Anderson's 1920 novel, *Poor White*.

influence, Hugh makes his first transition, becoming more active and materialistic. Though the change is generally for the better, Hugh also loses some of his ability to enjoy nature and live naturally.

From Mudcat Landing, Hugh goes to Bidwell, Ohio. Bidwell has sometimes been called a major character in the book. Even more than *Winesburg, Ohio*, *Poor White* is an examination of an Ohio town's evolution from an agricultural to an industrial focus. The change is simplified and symbolized in the course of Hugh's life: Lonely and unable to communicate, he begins tinkering with machines, finally producing labor-saving inventions such as a cabbage planter and a corn cutter. His inten-

tions are good, but he gives control to a selfish businessman, Steve Hunter. Thinking only of the good he wants to do for overworked farmers, Hugh does not realize that the factories are causing more harm than good. The factories employ foreign workers who live in shoddy housing while local workmen with outdated skills (one like Anderson's father, a harness maker) are driven to poverty. Greed and avarice corrupt the town, and a strict class system arises.

Hugh's second transformation comes when he overhears a group of workers curse him and Steve Hunter. Hugh develops a sense of moral maturity and a sympathy for those who have been displaced by the industrial age. He also recaptures some of the love of nature and beauty that he had lost. He meets Clara Butterworth, whose own psychological and ethical development is central to the novel. Clara is a strong woman who guides Hugh by her natural feminine understanding. Accepting neither restrictive morals nor industrial greed, she shows Hugh—and the reader—the corrupted natures of other characters, including that of her own father, Tom Butterworth.

When Hugh and Clara marry, Hugh is at first afraid to approach her, but Clara slowly helps him mature, both sexually and ethically. Finally Hugh gives up making machines, deciding to be a poet rather than an inventor. The couple's life is not ideal, but each has learned to live in the world and still behave with moral understanding. They hope for a better world for the next generation.

Analysis. Although *Poor White* is a cohesive novel in a way that *Winesburg, Ohio* is not, Anderson still has difficulty unifying the plot. The introduction of Clara's story breaks the narrative into two parts and interferes with the growing conflict in Hugh's own story. Moreover, the novel tends to summarize practical changes in the town and psychological changes in the characters, instead of describing them through specific actions or dialogue. Still, *Poor White* is among the most successful of Anderson's novels, due to both the complexity of the characters and the social and moral issues they face.

Poor White also deserves praise for its mixture of the real and the symbolic. While Bidwell is portrayed as a specific Ohio town, it also serves as a symbol of the changes in the United States, especially the Midwest, at the end of the nineteenth century. This theme of social and industrial change, which is interesting background in *Winesburg, Ohio*, is a central focus in *Poor White*. This focus also provides Anderson with an underlying structure for the book, as Hugh McVey's journey to manhood and greater understanding parallels the town's descent into greed, division of social classes, and mistreatment of workers. Anderson suggests

that the farmers could have used the relative freedom of their agrarian lifestyle to develop themselves intellectually and psychologically, but instead they chose to follow the temptations of industrialism, which led them in a worse direction.

The novel also explores a theme common in Anderson's writing: the isolation of people—especially men and women—from each other and the necessity of contact and communication. Hugh can barely propose marriage to Clara and, after their wedding, does not approach her sexually for days. His reticence is symbolic of an emotional wall between them that lasts until an unexpected trauma—an old tradesman's murderous attack on Hugh—helps to break it down.

SOURCES FOR FURTHER STUDY

Anderson, David D. "Sherwood Anderson's *Poor White* and the Grotesques Become Myth." *Midamerica* 14 (1987): 89–100.

Copenhaver, Eleanor. "Sherwood Anderson on *Poor White*." In *Sherwood Anderson: Centennial Studies*, edited by Hilbert H. Campbell et al. Troy, N.Y.: Whitston, 1976.

Ennis, Stephen. "Alienation and Affirmation: The Divided Self in Sherwood Anderson's *Poor White*." *South Atlantic Review* 55, no. 2 (May, 1990): 85–99.

Hoeber, Daniel R. "The 'Unkinging' of Man: Intellectual Background as Structural Device in Sherwood Anderson's *Poor White*." *South Dakota Review* 15 (1977): 45–60.

Rosenman, John B. "Anderson's *Poor White* and Faulkner's *Absalom, Absalom!*" *Mississippi Quarterly* 29 (1976): 437–438.

WINESBURG, OHIO

Genre: Novel
Subgenre: *Bildungsroman*, character sketches
Published: New York, 1919
Time period: 1890s
Setting: Small town in Ohio

Themes and Issues. Anderson often wrote in an autobiographical mode and mined his own adolescence for this story of coming-of-age in the Midwest as the region shifted from agriculture to industry. Anderson also explores the inner lives of the people in the fictional small town of Winesburg, Ohio, who are often spoiled by their frustrated desires, particularly the desire to communicate and connect with others. The book especially highlights moments of intense emotion and decision—moments that define a person's life. *Winesburg, Ohio* is also about storytelling and becoming a writer.

The Plot. The book begins with a somewhat mysterious introduction, referring to "The Book of the Grotesque," written by an old man. Two chapters, "Hands" and "Paper Pills," follow; these seem to be individual stories and clarify the meaning of "grotesque." Wing Biddlebaum in "Hands" and Doctor Reefy in "Paper Pills" are both sad, lonely people, haunted by past events and frustrated by their inability to communicate with those around them. By the end of the novel, it is obvious that *Winesburg, Ohio* is the "Book of the Grotesque" that the old man has written.

In the third chapter, George Willard, the young man who is the central focus of the novel, is introduced. The chapter describes George's parents, especially his mother, a strong but defeated woman much like Anderson's mother. George is portrayed as a caring but confused person; he wants to make something of his life but realizes he must leave his small town to do it.

The rest of the book develops two types of stories. Stories of the first type concern the townspeople, many of whom confide in George, eager to share their hidden secrets with another person. One of the most moving is "Godliness: A Tale in Four Parts," about the effects of religious fanaticism on three generations of one family. In "The Philosopher," Doctor Parcival tells George, "Everyone in the world is Christ and they are all crucified." In "The Untold Lie," one man confides to another about having gotten a woman pregnant; the other man wonders about his own marriage and remains silent, deciding anything he would say about marriage would be a lie. In many stories, the fear of a thing often helps to create it, and the repression of feelings causes them to break out in stronger, more unpredictable ways. For instance, Alice Hindman, in "Adventure," endures her asexual loneliness until she feels compelled to run naked in the rain.

Stories of the second type primarily concern George, as he grows as a writer and as a man. He works for the local paper, steadily becoming more self-assured as he learns about the lives of others. His encounters with women mix joy with awkwardness, and George sometimes unintentionally hurts women emotionally, as in "Nobody Knows"

Grant Wood's 1930 oil painting *Arnold Comes of Age* (Sheldon Memorial Art Gallery, Lincoln, Nebraska) mirrors the coming-of-age theme that is prevalent in so many of Anderson's works, particularly in his most famous work, *Winesburg, Ohio.*

Gale Stockwell's 1933 painting *Parkville, Main Street (Missouri)* depicts the small-town setting that Anderson was so adept at capturing in *Winesburg, Ohio.*

and "An Awakening." In "Sophistication," a late-night encounter with a woman promotes George's understanding of himself and others. He comes to the realization that a natural human loneliness is overcome only through genuine contact with others.

Finally, George leaves Ohio, as Anderson did, ready to write. The book ends saying that George's life in Winesburg "had become but a background on which to paint the dreams of his manhood." Clearly, George has become the old man of the introduction, giving voice to his own story and to those of the people who have shared with him.

Analysis. *Winesburg, Ohio* can be called a novel, particularly a *Bildungsroman*—a novel

about the protagonist's coming-of-age. It tells the story of George Willard, who reaches manhood during the course of the book. However, it could also be viewed as a collection of short stories, because many of the chapters that depict the stories of Winesburg's residents could be, and in fact have been, published separately as short stories.

The book's radical and experimental style influenced other twentieth-century writers, including Ernest Hemingway and William Faulkner. Anderson's word choice is primarily simple, almost like that of regular speech, but his words convey atmosphere and emotions in a precise, yet impressionistic, way. His depiction of the various characters is sympathetic and marked by keen insight. Anderson once said, "the true history of life is but a history of moments," and *Winesburg, Ohio* concentrates on those moments when feelings are intense and life-changing decisions are made.

In *Winesburg, Ohio* Anderson critically examines small-town life, showing its lack of opportunity and its conservatism, alongside its moments of innocence and joy. Communication is a main theme: Although people know each others' business too well, they keep vast secrets from each other, unable to speak about meaningful things. With decades of hindsight, Anderson also shows Winesburg as a town in transition, undergoing social and economic changes that may or may not benefit the town, and to which some characters are unable to adapt. The town is presented very realistically, with small references in different chapters following a consistent map.

Anderson also develops a specific meaning of the term "grotesque," which is explained in the first chapter. Each character has embraced one truth so vigorously, and bent his or her life around it, that the truth becomes a falsehood and the person becomes a grotesque exaggeration of it. Anderson implies that only a writer, open to all truths, can avoid this fate. Most of the characters demonstrate the concept of the grotesque; they are warped by an idea or value that they embrace or (especially in the case of women) have pushed on them. However, the grotesques are "not all horrible" and even display a kind of beauty for those who learn their secrets.

Winesburg, Ohio was published to mixed reviews. Many critics were repulsed by Anderson's frank treatment of sex and considered the book immoral. Others were impressed by the book's literary style and striking, original characters. In any case, the book made Anderson's reputation as a writer and is still taught in high schools and colleges.

SOURCES FOR FURTHER STUDY

Ferris, John H., ed. *Sherwood Anderson, Winesburg, Ohio: Text and Criticism.* New York: Penguin, 1977.

Gochberg, Donald. "Stagnation and Growth: The Emergence of George Willard." *Expression* 4 (Winter, 1960): 29–35.

McAleer, John J. "Christ Symbolism in *Winesburg, Ohio.*" *Discourse* 4 (Summer, 1961): 168–181.

Phillips, William L. "How Sherwood Anderson Wrote *Winesburg, Ohio.*" *American Literature* 23 (March, 1951): 7–30.

Other Works

"DEATH·IN THE WOODS" (1933). This short story, printed in *Death in the Woods and Other Stories,* is one of Sherwood Anderson's best. It is a complex tale about an old woman's death and its effect on those, especially the narrator, who see her body. Various versions of the story exist—three published in Anderson's lifetime and three more after his death—showing the care and refinement of Anderson's technique. The old woman who dies in the woods is one of Anderson's noteworthy and sympathetic grotesques. However, the main force of the story lies in the experience of the narrator, who sees the body and, decades later, still cannot forget it. Moreover, the narrator's adult self understands, as his young self did not, the importance of the event to his life and of its lesson regarding the natural cycle of death and life.

"THE EGG" (1920). "The Egg," published as "The Triumph of the Egg" in *Dial* (1920) and in *The Triumph of the Egg* in 1921, is probably Anderson's best-known short story. It has been widely anthologized in various languages, and its dramatic version (published in 1937) has been repeatedly performed. The protagonist of "The Egg" is a grotesque, a chicken farmer who

The egg, the focal point of Thomas Hart Benton's 1934 painting *Twelve Planes and a Single Egg*, represents the titles of Anderson's best-known short story, "The Egg," published in 1920, and his 1921 collection of impressions, *The Triumph of the Egg*.

now owns a restaurant and insists on showing his collection of preserved deformed chickens to his diners. Another of Anderson's stories of failed hopes and frustrations, "The Egg" also displays a kind of grim humor as narrated by the man's son. As a character, the protagonist is both ridiculous and moving.

"I WANT TO KNOW WHY" (1919). "I Want to Know Why" is a short story that was published in *Smart Set* magazine (1919) and in Anderson's collection *The Triumph of the Egg*. It is set in the late nineteenth century at a race-track and tells of adult tragedies and pain from a young man's point of view. The man's pure, simple love of horses contrasts with the complex and often degrading world around him, as he encounters confusing issues of sex, race, and money. He is baffled by adults who condemn a good, generous man for gambling and cannot see the beauty of the horses running. Finally, he is shocked to see a woman he admires standing by the window in a brothel. At times the young narrator's perspective seems too mature, but the story offers strong characterization and an intensely nonconformist moral stance.

KIT BRANDON (1936). This novel offers one of Anderson's best female characters, a creative dual narration, and social critique based on Anderson's experience as a newspaper owner and editor in Virginia. Modeled after an actual woman, Kit comes from a poor Appalachian family and runs away at fourteen to find an odd version of the American Dream. While working in a cotton mill, she begins to understand the oppression of the southern class structure. She takes various lovers, joins a bootlegging gang, and finally decides that money is far less important than genuine contact with other people. The story is told in two intertwined narratives, one by the author-narrator and one in which Kit tells her own story.

MANY MARRIAGES (1923). Most critics consider this novel an interesting failure. Certainly intriguing is the noted influence of psychoanalyst Sigmund Freud, including his theories about the harms of sexual repression. John Webster, the respectable owner of a small factory, falls in love with his secretary and realizes the dullness of his marriage and business life. Anderson was ahead of his time in his condemnation of materialism and in his suggestion that lust for money might be an unnatural replacement for lust and love for other people.

In a symbolically effective but highly unrealistic scene, Webster's wife and teenage daughter discover him walking around naked; still naked, he explains to both of them the importance of truth and the poisonous effect of inhibitions. He also tells them that he is leaving to live in another town with his secretary. The wife commits suicide, but the daughter gains a new sense of self-respect and freedom.

Many Marriages created a scandal upon its release, resulting in initially high sales. Although it is not one of Anderson's best-known works, and it tends toward moralizing speeches, the novel is actually very well structured.

MID-AMERICAN CHANTS (1918). Anderson began writing the poetry in this volume in 1916, influenced by Walt Whitman and the King James Bible. The free verse is loose, only occasionally showing the keen phrasing and broad, penetrating vision of Whitman's poems. The moral and social visions that Anderson depicts in these poems are their most interesting aspects. Anderson wished the poems to speak for all rural midwesterners, and they envision small towns freed from the industrial age, returning to a golden age of love, honest agricultural work, and close community. He also followed Whitman's lead in celebrating the

Henry Stull's 1893 oil-on-canvas painting *Domino's Futurity* (National Museum of Racing and Hall of Fame, Saratoga Springs, New York) reflects the setting and period of Anderson's *"I Want to Know Why,"* a short story about a young man's loss of innocence at a late-nineteenth-century racetrack.

body and the sexes, believing it one way to cure the repression and spiritual downfall he saw around him.

Resources

The bulk of Sherwood Anderson's papers are in the *Little Review* Collection at the University of Wisconsin-Madison. Others are in the Newberry Library in Chicago and Houghton Library at Harvard University. Other sources of interest to students of Sherwood Anderson include the following:

The Sherwood Anderson Foundation. The Sherwood Anderson Foundation was founded by Anderson's daughter, Marion, and other relatives as a nonprofit trust, using royalties from Anderson's books to provide grants for developing writers. The foundation's Web site has rules for grant competition and a list of past winners, as well as a history of the foundation, a chronology of Anderson's life, and other links. (http://www.urich.edu/~journalm/sahome.html)

The Sherwood Anderson Review. This semiannual jour-

nal contains critical and biographical essays on Anderson and his work, as well as book reviews and photos. The journal's Web site has a history of Anderson, archives of back issues, and subscription information. (http://www.urich.edu/~journalm/eagle.html)

The Sherwood Anderson Page. This Web site features information about and a tour of Clyde, Ohio, Anderson's hometown, which figured heavily in his fiction. (http://www.nwohio.com/clydeoh/sherwood.htm)

The Sherwood Anderson Collection. Virginia Tech's large collection of Anderson-related photos, manuscripts, and books is cataloged on line. (http://scholar2.lib.vt.edu/spec/anderson/main.htm)

BERNADETTE LYNN BOSKY

Maya Angelou

BORN: April 4, 1928, St. Louis, Missouri
IDENTIFICATION: Late-twentieth-century poet and autobiographer, who also has written plays and children's books, composed music, and directed and acted in stage and film productions.

Maya Angelou is one of the most admired and respected authors in contemporary American literature, especially valued for her perspective on the African American experience and for her achievements in humanizing her struggle as an African American woman to gain self-fulfillment and respect for herself and for all blacks. Tireless in her efforts to elevate the status of African Americans and to bring an end to racism and segregation, she has not sacrificed the principles of unity and mutual respect among the races. Both her life and her work demonstrate the value of persistence, enlightened social action, and community.

The Writer's Life

On April 4, 1928, Maya Angelou was born Marguerite Annie Johnson in St. Louis, Missouri, the second child of Vivian and Bailey Johnson. When she was three years old, she and her older brother Bailey, who called her Maya, were sent to their maternal grandmother, Annie Henderson, in Stamps, Arkansas. With her son Willie, the loving but strict Annie operated a grocery store that served the poor black community. From her, Angelou learned the principles of hard work, honesty, and religious faith.

Although Angelou's early years as a mother were troubled and unstable, her bond with her son was always strong and loving, as reflected in Michael Escoffery's 1996 painting *Mother and Son*.

Childhood. The children enjoyed the atmosphere of the store, did their chores faithfully, and excelled in school. Angelou read avidly and enjoyed watching the many characters who frequented the store. When she was seven, she and Bailey went to live again with their mother in St. Louis, Missouri. There, Angelou was raped by her mother's boyfriend. The man was tried and convicted but inexplicably released immediately after the trial. That same day, he was found kicked to death. Angelou felt that she had caused his death by lying at his trial, when she had testified about the details of what had happened. Afraid that others might die if she continued to talk, she vowed to remain silent and spoke to no one, except Bailey, for five years.

Young Adulthood. After returning to Stamps, Maya was eventually brought out of her shell of silence by Mrs. Flowers, a wealthy, educated black woman who encouraged her to read good literature and to be proud of her African American heritage. Angelou graduated from the eighth grade in 1940, and the following year she and Bailey rejoined their mother, who was now in California. When Vivian married a successful businessman, San Francisco became the family's new home, where Angelou attended high school and enjoyed the beauty of the city and the freedom of her new life.

Angelou by then had developed the independence and fiery temperament of her mother. While visiting her father in San Diego, Maya argued with his live-in girlfriend and took to the streets, finding shelter for a month in a junkyard. She returned to San Francisco and in 1944 fought racial prejudice to become the city's first black streetcar conductor. Soon after her high school graduation in 1945, a brief, unpleasant sexual encounter with a male classmate left her pregnant. Only sixteen, she nevertheless resolved to raise the child, whom she named Clyde (and later changed to Guy).

Angelou took a job as a cook in a creole café, but, after a brief love affair, she went to San Diego, worked as a waitress, and became a madam for a short time. Back in San Francisco, she was refused induction into the military because, five years earlier, she had attended a school suspected of communist ties. Always interested in dance, she teamed briefly with a partner and performed in small clubs. While working as a cook in Stockton, California, she was persuaded by a handsome lover to work as a prostitute in his Sacramento brothel. After a week, however, she quit to go to her ill mother. When she returned to Stockton for her son, she found that his babysitter had taken him to Bakersfield. Fortunately, Angelou was reunited with him there, but the experience made her realize that she had to change her ways.

A Budding Career.
Angelou moved back in with her mother and continued to search for stability, believing she had found it with Tosh Angelos, a young man of Greek ancestry whom she married in 1952. After only a year, however, the two divorced, and she found herself once again on her own. She modified her married name to Angelou, to make it sound more exotic, and took a job as an exotic dancer in a seedy club. She was soon performing as a Cuban, singing calypso songs at the Purple Onion. There followed a chance to perform in *Porgy and Bess* on its 1954–1955 tour of Europe and Africa. The respect Angelou re-

Angelou is pictured above with writer Langston Hughes in October of 1958. She joined the Harlem Writer's Guild not long after this picture was taken.

ceived on the tour gave her increased confidence and sense of worth, but the months away from Guy were too heavy a price to pay, and she left the company to return to him.

Growing Stature.
The late 1950s atmosphere of social change in America aroused in Angelou a desire to move with the times. She went to Los Angeles, then to New York in 1959, where she joined the Harlem Writers Guild and became involved in civil rights activities. After hearing Martin Luther King, Jr., speak, she and her friend Godfrey Cambridge wrote and produced a play called *Cabaret for Freedom* (1960) to aid King's movement financially. In the same year, she appeared in a New York production of Jean Genet's *The Blacks* (1960).

Angelou's growing reputation as an organizer won her a job as head of the New York office of the

HIGHLIGHTS IN ANGELOU'S LIFE

1928	Maya Angelou is born Marguerite Johnson on April 4 in St. Louis, Missouri.
1931	Angelou is sent with her older brother Bailey to live with their grandmother in Stamps, Arkansas, when parents divorce.
1936	Angelou is raped by mother's boyfriend; stops speaking for five years.
1940	Graduates as a top student from the eighth grade in Stamps.
1941	Moves to San Francisco with her mother, now remarried; takes evening classes in drama and dance.
1944	Angelou is hired as first African American conductor on San Francisco streetcar line.
1945	Graduates from high school; gives birth to son, Clyde, whose name is later changed to Guy.
1946	Begins series of jobs as waitress, creole cook, and dancer.
1949	Becomes an exotic dancer in San Francisco nightclubs.
1952	Marries Tosh Angelos, whom she divorces a year later.
1954	Begins yearlong tour of Europe and North Africa with production of *Porgy and Bess*.
1959	Moves to New York to become a writer.
1960	Performs in Jean Genet's *The Blacks*; writes and produces *Cabaret for Freedom* with Godfrey Cambridge.
1961	Marries Vusumzi Make; moves to Cairo, Egypt; becomes associate editor of the *Arab Observer*.
1963	Leaves Make and moves to Ghana; works as assistant administrator at the University of Ghana; writes for the *Ghanian Times* while Guy attends classes.
1966	Returns to the United States.
1968	Narrates *Black, Blues, Black*, a ten-part series on African traditions in American life, for National Educational Television.
1970	Publishes *I Know Why the Caged Bird Sings*; is writer-in-residence at the University of Kansas and a Yale University fellow.
1971	Publishes *Just Give Me a Cool Drink of Water 'fore I Diiie*, which is nominated for Pulitzer Prize; adapts *I Know Why the Caged Bird Sings* for television.
1974	Publishes *Gather Together in My Name*; is distinguished visiting professor at Wake Forest University, Winston-Salem, North Carolina.
1975	Publishes *Oh Pray My Wings Are Gonna Fit Me Well*.
1976	Named Woman of the Year by the *Ladies Home Journal*; publishes *Singin' and Swingin' and Gettin' Merry Like Christmas*.
1981	Receives a lifetime appointment as Reynolds Professor of American Studies at Wake Forest University.
1986	Publishes *All God's Children Need Traveling Shoes*.
1993	Reads at the inauguration of President Clinton; publishes *Wouldn't Take Nothing for My Journey Now*.
1995	Gives readings at the United Nations and at the Million Man March in Washington, D.C.

Southern Christian Leadership Conference. This position brought her close to prominent people involved with racial issues both in the United States and Africa. One of those people was an African freedom fighter, Vusumzi Make, whose charm and intelligence won her heart.

Angelou married Vusumzi in 1961, and the couple moved to Cairo, Egypt. There Angelou donned the traditional sari, learned some Arabic, and developed close friendships. She also found a job as an associate editor for the *Arab Observer*. However, unable to tolerate an unfaithful husband, she left Vusumzi in 1963, taking another newspaper job in Liberia. On a stop in Ghana, Guy was seriously injured in an automobile accident, and Angelou settled there, working at the university and writing for the *Ghanian Times*. As her teenage son became more independent of her, Angelou felt increasingly out of place in Africa, sensing that she had absorbed all that the continent could give her.

Angelou conveys her hope for the future in her poem "On the Pulse of Morning" at President Bill Clinton's inauguration in Washington, D.C., on January 20, 1993.

Maturity. After returning to the United States, Angelou gained national prominence with the publication of her first autobiographical book, *I Know Why the Caged Bird Sings,* in 1970. Four other volumes of autobiography and several volumes of poetry followed, as well as television and film work. In 1981 Angelou received a lifetime appointment as Reynolds Professor of American Studies at Wake Forest University in Winston-Salem, North Carolina, where she would teach while continuing to speak nationwide on racial issues.

Awards and Honors. By 1993 Angelou had received fifty honorary degrees and was making eighty appearances a year as a lecturer. In the same year, she was invited to read a poem at the inauguration of President Bill Clinton. That poem, "On the Pulse of Morning," spoke for Angelou personally and for the nation. In it, her past, the nation's past, and the future of both were united in an expression of fresh hope.

The Writer's Work

In both her prose and poetry, Maya Angelou emphasizes the value of the individual, irrespective of gender or race. Throughout her childhood in the segregated South and in California, she struggled against racial prejudice while striving to achieve a sense of self-worth and self-fulfillment. Her private struggles and mental growth have coincided with the social changes of the past forty years, in which she herself has played an important part. Her journey through hardship to eventual triumph is recorded with candor and detail in her five autobiographical works and in her poetry. Her writings focus on overcoming obstacles, living with dignity and self-respect, and enlightening oneself and others.

Issues and Themes in Angelou's Writing.

As Angelou herself has noted, she uses themes to select the material of her autobiographies. She would think of a subject, such as cruelty, kindness, or generosity, and then would select incidents in her life to illustrate these ideas. A common thread that runs through all of her autobiographies is the suffering caused by racism. Angelou explores this theme through the eyes of an African American woman who is, in much of her life, a single mother struggling to raise a child, to earn a living, to develop a career, and to achieve self-understanding. She gives this focus wide significance by infusing her struggles against both racism and sexism with an independent spirit and clear sense of

Reverend Martin Luther King, Jr., greeting his parishioners outside the Ebenezer Baptist Church in Atlanta, Georgia, after Sunday services on November 8, 1964. As Angelou's appreciation of the individual worth grew stronger, King's message of love and his nonviolent approach increasingly appealed to her.

Angelou in San Francisco around 1970, the year *I Know Why the Caged Bird Sings* was published.

the value of her effort. Her humanity and modesty ennoble her work.

At the heart of virtually all of Angelou's writing is an opposition to racism and the justice of the African American struggle for equality. Her career bears the influence of black leaders such as Malcolm X, who preached aggressive militancy, and Martin Luther King, Jr., who preached nonviolent resistance, brotherly love, and racial harmony. When Angelou first became politically active, she leaned toward the militancy of Malcolm X. Over the years, however, her more radical views became modified by her strong regard for the value of the individual, regardless of race, color, or nationality.

Angelou's Poetry. Although Angelou's literary reputation rests solidly on her autobiographies, she is also known as an accomplished poet. Her poetry represents a natural combination of her love of language, her ear for the rhythms of speech, and her musical talent. In her childhood, she would recite poetry to herself, not liking it until she could feel it with her tongue and lips. Sound and rhythm, for her, are extremely important, and she has written verse throughout her adult life.

Many critics believe that Angelou's greatest strength lies in her prose, and this thinking is evident in the criticism about her work, the vast majority of which discusses only her autobiographies, ignoring her poetry. However, Angelou's poetry merits praise for its control of language and its way with speech patterns, particularly those associated with African American culture. Her poetry contains the same energy and liveliness found in her prose but reflects graceful style, sharp imagery, and skillful use of sound.

The poetic genre has enabled Angelou to step out of the confines of prose rhythms and to employ a wider range of musical effects. She said that she begins with a rhythm, into which she tries to fit the content of her poem. Without the prose requirements of thematic development and narrative unity, Angelou is able to discuss personal feelings and experiences lyrically, capturing brief moments of

Black militant leader Malcolm X speaking at a rally in Harlem on May 14, 1963, in support of integration measures in Birmingham, Alabama. Believing in the justice of the African American struggle for equality, Angelou found herself influenced by Malcolm X during her earlier years as an activist.

SOME INSPIRATIONS BEHIND ANGELOU'S WORK

Early in her life, Maya Angelou read the work of William Shakespeare and was especially drawn to his Sonnet 29, which expresses her own sense of isolation, rejection, and sorrow. She was also greatly impressed with early twentieth-century African American poet Paul Laurence Dunbar, whose poetry, often in dialect, records life in the African American community. The title of her first autobiography is from one of Dunbar's poems.

Angelou was mesmerized by the rhythms and imagery of the black ministers she heard in her Arkansas childhood. Their preaching left an indelible mark on her mind and helped shape her literary character, as did the spontaneous emotional outbursts of members of the congregation. She sought to enliven her own writing with the powerful effect of strong emotion, expressed in rhythmic, highly individual language.

By the time Angelou began writing, she was already familiar with the work of many authors, and she returned to them repeatedly. She continued to be influenced into adulthood by the lyrical language of the Bible, incorporating its rhythms and sounds into her own writing. The Bible's influence extends also to her thinking, especially its emphasis on love rather than hate.

Other authors helped to shape Angelou's prose, including James Weldon Johnson, particularly in his *Autobiography of an Ex-Colored Man* (1912). Her autobiographies have been influenced by the writing of Frederick Douglass, who established the genre of the first-person slave narrative.

Angelou has mentioned several other authors, including Edgar Allan Poe and Matthew Arnold, whose work taught her to appreciate the music of language and elevated expression. Angelou gives special credit to a particular novel, *Dom Casmurro* (1899), by the Brazilian author Joachim Maria Machado de Assis, which taught her to see natural beauty more clearly and inspired her attempt to do the same with her own story. After reading that novel several times, she began writing her first book.

Angelou reads one of her works at the dedication of the Millennium Village at Walt Disney World in Orlando, Florida, in September 1999.

mood, thought, and feeling with the compression that only poetry allows. Poetry also enables her to explore the possibilities of line length, sound effects, and other aspects of language use not available to traditional prose.

These aspects of Angelou's creative use of language are amply illustrated in her poems, which offer a different perspective on the subjects and themes found in her prose. Angelou favors the short poem, under fifty lines, and avoids narrative poetry. Most of her poems have rhyme, usually end-rhyme, but sometimes internal rhyme. Her lines tend to be short, containing three or four stresses, and often only one or two. Stanzas, too, are rela-

tively short, four to ten lines, and have irregular patterns. These structures concentrate the content into brief lyrical statements that depend primarily on sound and rhythm, including a frequent use of the refrain and infrequently on imagery.

On the whole, Angelou's poetry is linear, graceful, and always clear. Angelou is not interested in formal obscurity, convoluted grammar, or omissions that require the reader to guess at her meaning. She wants to be understood, and this desire is part of her commitment to connecting with people immediately and easily. She is as candid in her poetry as she is in her autobiographies, but her poetic emo-

Angelou singing with clergyman Cecil Williams (right) at the Glide Memorial Methodist Church in San Francisco, California, on Sunday, July 14, 1974.

tions derive from personal feelings that seem closer to her heart than to her mind. The result is a surface simplicity that has been mistaken for lack of depth.

Angelou has said that she tries hard to condense her ideas and feelings into their most succinct forms. Sometimes fifteen pages of notes result in only four lines of verse. The simplicity of Angelou's poems compliments the reader and emphasizes the musical quality of her thought and feeling.

Angelou's subjects mirror her prose, discussing both private and public subjects. Several poems celebrate the sensual aspects of love, loneliness, and the search for a companion. Angelou writes of growing old, of friends and relatives. Social consciousness is evident in several poems that speak of black pride, war, welfare, and drug use.

Angelou's Literary Legacy.

Angelou was not the first writer to use autobiography to shed light on the black experience. Frederick Douglass's *Narrative of the Life of Frederick Douglass, an American Slave, Written by Himself* (1845) exposed the horrors of slavery, and both Richard Wright, in *Native Son* (1940), and Ralph Ellison, in *Invisible Man* (1952), used fictional autobiography to call attention to the plight of the African American man. Angelou continues the tradition, using autobiography to keep issues of racism and segregation in the national eye.

Because of Angelou's efforts, African American writers, and especially female writers, have gained wider acceptance and greater respectability. Her vividness and veracity have given added impetus to the struggle for equality. She richly and movingly records the African American experience from the early days of the Civil Rights movement to the present day.

In her lectures, Angelou brings to public attention the many and important contributions that African Americans have made to American culture. To her, the African American woman epitomizes the will to survive without losing compassion. Like Angelou herself, the archetypal black female represents inclusiveness, though she has often been excluded from mainstream America. Her greatest legacy lies in her ability to infuse universality into her experience, giving her highly praised work an importance that goes beyond racial and gender concerns. Because they speak about important issues in such compelling ways, Angelou's books continue to be used in American studies and women's studies classes.

This photograph of Angelou on a San Francisco beach was used to promote her 1978 book of poems, *And Still I Rise*.

BIBLIOGRAPHY

Andrews, William L., ed. *African-American Autobiography: A Collection of Critical Essays.* Englewood Cliffs, N.J.: Prentice Hall, 1993.

Gates, Henry Louis, Jr. *Reading Black, Reading Feminist: A Critical Anthology.* New York: Meridian, 1990.

Jelinek, Estelle C., ed. *Women's Autobiography: Essays in Criticism.* Bloomington: Indiana University Press, 1980.

King, Sarah E. *Greeting the Morning: Maya Angelou.* Brookfield, Conn.: Millbrook Press, 1994.

Lupton, Mary Jane. *Maya Angelou: A Critical Companion.* Westport, Conn.: Greenwood Press, 1998.

Pettit, Jayne. *Maya Angelou: Journey of the Heart.* New York: Lodestar Books, 1996.

Shapiro, Miles. *Maya Angelou.* Philadelphia: Chelsea House, 2000.

Showalter, Elaine, ed. *Modern American Women Writers.* New York: Charles Scribner's Sons, 1991.

Shuker, Nancy. *Maya Angelou.* Englewood Cliffs, N.J.: Simon & Schuster, 1990.

Williams, Mary E., ed. *Readings on Maya Angelou.* San Diego, Calif.: Greenhaven Press, 1997.

NONFICTION

1970   I Know Why the Caged Bird Sings (autobiography)

1974   Gather Together in My Name (autobiography)

1976   Singin' and Swingin' and Gettin' Merry Like Christmas (autobiography)

1981   The Heart of a Woman (autobiography)

1986   All God's Children Need Traveling Shoes (autobiography)

1993   Wouldn't Take Nothing for My Journey Now (autobiographical essays)

1997   Even the Stars Look Lonesome (essays)

PLAY

1960   Cabaret for Freedom (with Godfrey Cambridge)

POETRY

1971   Just Give Me a Cool Drink of Water 'fore I Diiie

1975   Oh Pray My Wings Are Gonna Fit Me Well

1978   And Still I Rise

1983   Shaker, Why Don't You Sing?

1986   Poems: Maya Angelou

1987   Now Sheba Sings the Song (with art by Tom Feelings)

1990   I Shall Not Be Moved: Poems

1993   On the Pulse of Morning

1994   The Complete Collected Poems of Maya Angelou

1994   Phenomenal Woman: Four Poems Celebrating Women

1995   A Brave and Startling Truth

CHILDREN'S LITERATURE

1993   Life Doesn't Frighten Me (with paintings by Jean-Michel Basquiat)

1994   My Painted House, My Friendly Chicken, and Me (with photographs by Margaret Courtney-Clarke)

1996   Kofi and His Magic (with photographs by Courtney-Clarke)

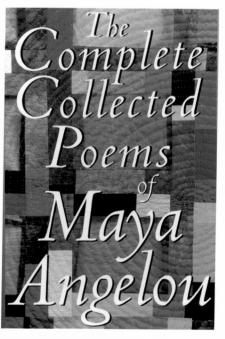

Maya Angelou's Universal Appeal

Maya Angelou has said that she has tried to bring a special quality to her writing, particularly to her autobiographies. Although conscious of writing in the tradition of Frederick Douglass, Ralph Ellison, and other famous African American writers, she has sought to give her work universal significance. She does not write simply of her own emotions. Rather, she incorporates the emotions of all her readers into the story she tells by instilling into her first-person, singular narrative the universality of the third-person "we."

Universal Themes. Part of Angelou's strategy is to select her material according to its universal value, first selecting a theme, such as envy or kindness, and then building episodes from her life around it. In this process of transference, Angelou alters facts and characters to create the essential truths of her experience and of universal experience. Her autobiographies thus become artful arrangements with wide-ranging appeal.

Angelou poses at the Grammy Awards in 1994 at Radio City Music Hall in New York with her Grammy for Best Spoken Word or Nontraditional Album, which she won for the recording of "On the Pulse of Morning."

Angelou with pen and paper in hand in 1994. Although she has been a singer, a dancer, and a political activist at various points in her life, she has often said that writing is her greatest joy.

Angelou uses the techniques of the novelist, such as rich detail, dramatic scenes, and vivid characters, to give the truth of her experience greater effect. She strives to make readers feel her experience and to see their own feelings in hers. The vivid imagery and the power of her rhythms show readers her truths and allow them to live in her work. The wide popularity of Angelou's prose and poetry, and the praise it has received from readers, is evidence of her success.

Character and Action. Critics have admired Angelou's skill in depicting scenes that are alive with character and action. These skills easily translate into material for stage and film, and Angelou has produced many works for both. Her lifelong love of reading and reciting poetry, as well as her experiences as a dancer and singer, prepared her well for capturing and expressing the sounds and rhythms of human speech. Both her personal difficulties as a single teenage mother and her political activism in the struggle for racial and gender equality provided the material of her writing, and her desire to speak to others and to be a great writer in the tradition of Frederick Douglass gave her the energy to produce such a large body of well-received literature.

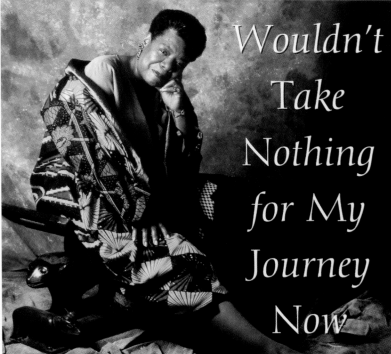

This photograph of Angelou, which graces the cover of Bantam's 1997 edition of her book of essays *Wouldn't Take Nothing for My Journey Now,* was taken in 1997 by photographer Dwight Carter.

Love of Language. Much of the power of Angelou's writing comes from her love of language. By her own count, she is more or less proficient in seven or eight languages, including French, Spanish, Italian, Arabic, and Fanti (a language of Ghana, a west African country). Angelou is fascinated by the nuances of sound and meaning and the rhythm of sentence. English remains her favorite language, however, and she takes great care to make it work best for her. Two of her constant companions as she writes are a thesaurus and the Bible. Her own reading taught her that how something is said is essential to its success in gaining readers' participation and in making a lasting impression. Truth, for Angelou, is in the writer's honesty of expression, and must be well crafted to live in readers' minds. Craft, to her, is as important as insight.

Civil Rights Struggle. Angelou came of age at a time in history when the struggle against American racial segregation began to accelerate, and leaders such as Malcolm X and Martin Luther King, Jr., gained national attention, power, and respect. Angelou played a small but important role in that history as an activist; she played a much greater role as an author whose literature recorded and fueled the struggle. She and her work have provided a voice for the African American community and an inspiration to others to speak and to write. Indeed, Angelou's reputation and achievements cannot be separated from the history of African American suffering and struggle in the second half of the twentieth century. Angelou has come to symbolize the best of the struggle for racial equality and is admired for her ability to rise above hatred and the narrow perspective of race, speaking for all those who seek equality and justice. A high point in this effort came when she was asked to deliver a poem at the inauguration of President Bill Clinton in 1993.

Despite her popularity as a public figure, Angelou is foremost a writer. Writing, she has said many times, is her greatest joy and outlet. It is also her greatest strength, and although she writes primarily about issues associated with racism, her work rises above her personal experience and particular events as she explores such universal themes as striving for self-understanding and self-fulfillment, overcoming obstacles, and needing others. Ultimately, Angelou aims in her work to bring understanding and to unite people. She wants people to know that despite their personal failings, they are more alike than not and that they do need one another.

SOURCES FOR FURTHER STUDY

Estes-Hicks, Onita. "The Way We Were: Precious Memories of the Black Segregated South." *African American Review* 27, no. 1 (Spring 1993): 9–18.

Harper, Judith E. *Maya Angelou*. Chanhassen, Minn.: Child's World, 1999.

Loos, Pamela. *Maya Angelou*. Philadelphia: Chelsea House, 2000.

Reader's Guide to Major Works

ALL GOD'S CHILDREN NEED TRAVELING SHOES

Genre: Autobiography
Subgenre: Domestic realism
Published: 1986
Time period: 1962 to 1965
Setting: Ghana, Africa

Themes and Issues. One of the themes in this fifth volume of Maya Angelou's autobiography is the search for a true and lasting home. In a broad sense, home may be found in the soli-darity represented by the Black Power move-ment. More specifically, it is represented by marriage and Africa, both as an ideal and as a geographical entity. At last, in the country of her ancestors, Angelou searches for a perma-nent place that is both spiritual and physical.

The Plot. As the book begins, Angelou be-lieves that marriage to an African freedom fighter might provide a lasting, ideal home for herself and her son. When her marriage fails, she settles in Ghana and joyfully discovers that

In her 1986 autobiography, *All God's Children Need Traveling Shoes*, Angelou expresses the importance of family and community, both of which are depicted in Allan Rohan Crite's 1936 painting *School's Out* (The Smithsonian American Art Museum).

Africans live there the way whites do in the United States. She feels a shared heritage with black Africans, and, for the first time in her life, she is at home in a community of blacks who are not segregated or oppressed because of the color of their skin.

In time, Angelou is dismayed to discover that discrimination exists even among African blacks: She and her fellow immigrants are considered outsiders by native Africans. This experience is a sobering reminder that she and all African Americans are displaced, at home neither in Africa nor in America. Although Angelou feels among the world's homeless, she concludes at the book's end that because her own roots are in the United States, she must belong there. Her sense of self-worth and racial equality demands equal respect and equal treatment. Ultimately, she realizes that home is within, wherever one is.

Over the course of this volume, Angelou overcomes major limitations in her own life, among them hatred and distrust of whites, and achieves independence and self-understanding. She rises to a point where she does not let events control her but instead controls them. While nurturing her own individuality, she labors constantly to bring people together. To achieve this understanding takes a willingness to move—intellectually, emotionally, and geographically—and to meet people of all types. The individual on the move needs shoes, an idea conveyed by the book's title. The responsible individual needs to travel, both literally and figuratively, in order to discover the ultimate truth: that the only true home is within oneself.

Analysis. In all her autobiographies, Angelou reveals both directly and indirectly the family's importance to the development of the individual. The idea that family—and, in a larger meaning, community—is essential to the value of the individual is but one theme that emerges in Angelou's experiences. Her increasing political involvement, which sets her apart from other members of her family, also makes her a member of the larger community of activists.

Angelou's autobiographies take on an increasingly broad significance as she grows intellectually. The unifying element throughout this volume is the conviction that people must fight for their beliefs and for what they want to achieve. They need to create a sense of family by forming close ties with others, and all races need to work together to make a world in which all people can live in harmony.

SOURCES FOR FURTHER STUDY

McPherson, Dolly A. *Order out of Chaos: The Autobiographical Works of Maya Angelou.* New York: Peter Lang, 1990.

Olney, James. *Metaphors of Self: The Meaning of Autobiography.* Princeton, N.J.: Princeton University Press, 1972.

O'Neale, Sondra. "Reconstruction of the Composite Self: New Images of Black Women in Maya Angelou's Continuing Autobiography." In *Black Women Writers (1950–1980): A Critical Evaluation,* edited by Mari Evans. New York: Anchor Press/Doubleday, 1983.

I KNOW WHY THE CAGED BIRD SINGS

Genre: Autobiography
Subgenre: Domestic realism
Published: New York, 1970
Time period: 1930s and early 1940s
Setting: Missouri; Arkansas; California

Themes and Issues. Discovery is a major theme of this first volume of Angelou's autobiography. Much of the book's emotional force comes from Angelou's descriptions of her sense of unworthiness and her search for self-identity. A parallel theme is that of her growing resentment of racial segregation and its effects. While Angelou admires her grandmother's moral strength and dignity in the face of racial prejudice, she struggles with her own confused emotions. Southern racism determined the course of her life by giving her a focus, a cause, and a consciousness that unify every aspect of her life and work. Another important theme that emerges from this first volume and runs through all of the volumes is the importance of family and familial relationships.

The Plot. This book traces Angelou's life from her early days in Stamps, Arkansas, to the birth of her son in San Francisco when she was sixteen. In the intervening thirteen years, she was raped while living with her mother in St. Louis, Missouri; graduated from the eighth grade in Stamps, Arkansas; and moved to San Francisco, California, where her mother had remarried and made a new home.

As the book begins, Angelou and her brother, Bailey, are sent to live with their maternal grandmother in Arkansas, while their mother stays in Missouri. Both children are conscious of their mother's absence, fearing that she does not love them. To fill the gap, they turn to Annie Henderson, whom they address as Momma, and who serves as their mother through much of their childhood. Uncle Willie and other men serve as surrogate fathers.

The family provides not only companionship but also protection. Many scenes show family members protecting one another. Throughout Angelou's childhood, Bailey is her companion and protector, and when the man who raped her in St. Louis is found beaten to death, the implication is that Angelou's uncles are responsible. A broader sense of community among other African Americans overlaps these important close family relationships.

Analysis. Angelou's first book is noteworthy for its masterful handling of character and ac-

William H. Johnson's oil painting *Lift Up Thy Voice and Sing* (Smithsonian American Art Museum), ca. 1944, captures the strong sense of community and the power of song that are evident in Angelou's 1970 autobiography, *I Know Why the Caged Bird Sings*.

tion, combining the vividness of the best fiction with the power of personal history to create unforgettable scenes. Among her finest achievements are her sensitive but unsentimental depictions of the segregated lives of African Americans.

A church scene, for example, is described in a way that shows the people as humans rather than stereotypes: "Another holler went up in front of me, and a large woman flopped over, her arms above her head like a candidate for baptism." The scene unfolds in riotous detail, rising to the climactic singing and chanting of the congregation that reaches feverish heights. When Angelou comments, "They basked in the righteousness of the poor and the exclusiveness of the downtrodden," she could be talking about anyone anywhere who is poor and downtrodden, but she brings her narrative back to her theme by quoting a member of the congregation: "Let the whitefolks have their money and power and segregation and sarcasm and big houses and schools and lawns like carpets, and books, and mostly—mostly—let them have their whiteness." The chanting voices of the overwrought congregation become one of the book's most moving moments.

SOURCES FOR FURTHER STUDY

Bloom, Harold, ed. *Maya Angelou's "I Know Why the Caged Bird Sings."* Philadelphia: Chelsea House, 1998.

Kent, George E. "Maya Angelou's *I Know Why the Caged Bird Sings* and Black Autobiographical Tradition." *Kansas Quarterly* 7 (Summer 1975).

Smith, Sidonie Ann. "The Song of a Caged Bird: Maya Angelou's Quest for Self-Acceptance." *Southern Humanities Review* 7 (Fall 1973).

SINGIN' AND SWINGIN' AND GETTIN' MERRY LIKE CHRISTMAS

Genre: Autobiography
Subgenre: Domestic realism
Published: New York, 1976
Time period: 1949 to 1955
Setting: California; Europe; Africa

Themes and Issues. Angelou's third autobiographical volume follows her quest for self-fulfillment and her increasing concern with issues of racism and segregation. She further develops her professional identity as that of a black female performer, and her work places her among black performers and celebrities who, like her, are determined to combat racism and segregation.

The Plot. In this volume, Angelou enters a world far different from the sordid settings of her second history, *Gather Together in My Name*. Her son, Guy, is now five years old. Early in the narrative, Angelou marries a kind, decent man who loves her son and provides a stable home life. Her dream is shattered, though, when, after a year, her husband requests a divorce.

Once again Angelou is a single mother struggling to make a living. This time, however, her life takes a very different turn: She becomes an exotic dancer and discovers that her looks—she is by now six feet tall, slim, and attractive—and talent are genuine assets. Her fortunes rapidly improve, and she is soon performing in a traveling production of *Porgy and Bess* with a prestigious group of professional actors, traveling in Europe, and being accepted as an equal by all.

Her developing career as a singer and dancer, however, prevents Angelou from being the excellent mother she wants to be, and this book records her increasing guilt and conflict. In addition, the death of her grandmother and the loss of closeness with her brother Bailey intensify her sense of isolation. However, her story ends in triumph when she leaves the touring cast of *Porgy and Bess* and returns to her son.

Analysis. The spirited title of this volume highlights the mood of the narrative. Angelou arrives at an understanding of her own value as a woman, mother, performer, and activist. Success in show business shows her that she can make a living for herself and her son. She also finds direction and a way out of the trap of racism in which many African Americans have found themselves.

In her personal life, which is rarely separate from her public life, Angelou finds a renewed sense of purpose: to be the best mother she can be. She decides she will never again separate herself from her son, who has given her a better understanding of herself, a deeper sense of her value, and a presence that completely satisfies her need to nurture. As she moves into the world of professionals on an international scale, her contacts with whites also increase; she goes from distrust and hatred of all whites to a tentative acceptance and trust of those who treat her with respect.

The narrative opens with a series of scenes establishing this shift in Angelou's perspective. When the owner of a record store becomes very friendly, Angelou is suspicious, adding: "It wasn't wise to reveal one's real feelings to strangers. And nothing on earth was stranger to me than a friendly white woman." When the woman offers her a job, Angelou "pried into her eyes for hidden meaning and found nothing. Even so, I had to show my own strength." She accepts the job, and her icy reserve and distrust melt away. Later, in Europe, she can look freely at whites and gains a new perspective on them. Gone are her adolescent naïveté and moral blindness. In their place Angelou presents a strong-minded and intelligent central character who is in control of her thoughts and emotions, has a firm grasp of reality, and is willing to change her beliefs as a result of her experience. From time to time, she describes her performing talents and her looks as simply good enough, although the attention she receives from audiences and fellow professionals suggests otherwise. This modesty is sustained as her fortunes improve and reflects a maturity not found in her earlier books.

The book's narrative design is determined by the resolution of Angelou's racial attitudes—her mental and emotional growth—and by the resolution of her conflict between career and motherhood. The book begins with a marriage that, despite its failure, reflects a profound and positive change in Angelou's thinking. Toward the end of the book, with her independence and career well established, Angelou cannot re-

This photograph of Angelou was taken for an album cover around 1960.

solve career and motherhood. The conflict leads to a mental breakdown, and she considers suicide. A friend convinces her that she has much for which to be thankful and for which to live. She realizes that her achievements have come out of herself, her talents, her intelligence, and her hard work. She has value, and she controls her destiny.

When her son announces that he has changed his name from Clyde to Guy, recovers from a severe rash, and begins once more to tell her his secrets, Angelou sees a "physical and mental metamorphosis" in him that issues from her own transformation. Once again, her son has given closure to an important chapter in her life and has opened another.

SOURCES FOR FURTHER STUDY

Olney, James, ed. *Autobiography: Essays Theoretical and Critical.* Princeton, N.J.: Princeton University Press, 1980.

Porter, Roger, and H. R. Wolf. *The Voice Within: Reading and Writing Autobiography.* New York: Knopf, 1973.

Weintraub, Karl Joachim. *The Value of the Individual Self and Circumstance in Autobiography.* Chicago: University of Chicago Press, 1978.

Other Works

THE COMPLETE COLLECTED POEMS OF MAYA ANGELOU (1994).

Maya Angelou's first volume of poetry, *Just Give Me a Cool Drink of Water 'fore I Diiie,* published in 1971, was nominated for a Pulitzer Prize. Several other volumes of poetry followed. *The Complete Collected Poems of Maya Angelou* contains all of her published poems up to 1994, including "On the Pulse of Morning," the poem she read at the inauguration of President Bill Clinton.

Angelou often uses African American dialect in her poetry, not to make fun or ridicule, but to capture the actual vocabulary, grammar, and rhythms of speech. Dialect can have great evocative power, as in her poem "Little Girl Speakings," in which a child defends her mother, using language to express herself: "No lady cookinger than my Mommy, smell that pie, see I don't lie, No lady cookinger than my Mommy."

In that one word, "cookinger," Angelou conveys a world of feeling and a struggle to be heard, no matter the cost to "correct" English. The child's social circumstances are implied as well in her contorted vocabulary. The lines show her triumph—she succeeds in expressing her feelings; to the extent that she represents the black population, her triumph becomes theirs, too. This child evokes a sympathy and admiration for her courage and inventiveness: She finds a way to express her feelings despite a limited vocabulary, ultimately achieving greater expression.

GATHER TOGETHER IN MY NAME (1974).

In her second autobiographical volume, Angelou highlights her struggle to find ways to be an excellent mother to her son, a struggle that takes her into show business, leads to the loss of her innocence, and sharpens her understanding of her life goals. Her determination to fend for herself, often without clear direction, mingles both courage and naïveté with a willingness to try just about anything to make a decent life for herself and her son. All the while, she never loses her conviction that racial prejudice is unjust and that truth is her best support.

As she strays from her moral center, Angelou loses touch with reality, risking her safety, health, and freedom—to say nothing of her relationship with her son—to achieve an imaginary goal. She paces the reader through her downward journey with masterful control.

The book's climactic scene is also the lowest point in Angelou's descent and a turning point

William H. Johnson's painting *Little Sweet* (Smithsonian American Art Museum) reflects the innocence Angelou regains and cherishes in her 1974 autobiography, *Gather Together in My Name*.

in her growth. A male friend for whom Angelou fences stolen women's clothing is a heroin addict. As she watches him inject the drug into his arm, he invites her to join him. Poised on the brink, Angelou is prepared to accept his offer, but her friend decides for her, making her promise never to take the drug. She backs away, and in doing so, regains control of her life. She rediscovers her innocence and how much it means to her.

THE HEART OF A WOMAN (1981). A mature and self-aware Angelou broadens her vision in her fourth autobiographical volume. Angelou continues to weave together in seamless fashion her public and private lives, shifting from one to the other with graceful ease. She notes the social changes stirring in American society of the 1950s and 1960s and subtly conveys a sense of her own stature as a performer and writer and activist in the Civil Rights movement. She is surrounded by other African American artists and writers and is respected as an actress, activist, writer, and editor.

When Angelou meets Vusumzi Make, the African freedom fighter whom she marries and accompanies to Egypt, she discovers that Africa is moving, too. Another profound change in her life is her decision to give up show business. She has long sought emotional depth and intellectual growth, and, in her move to Africa, she achieves both.

Angelou writes with modulated, temperate language to retell even the most volatile events in a reflection of her own hard-won self-control. She describes an encounter with a gang leader who has threatened Guy and matter-of-factly explains her initial attempt to understand the young man's thinking. This understated beginning rises to a tense, climactic moment, in which she warns the gang leader: "If the Savages so much as touch my son, I will then find your house and kill everything that moves, including the rats and cockroaches." She then shows the young man the pistol she carries in her purse.

Such scenes portray a woman who can face down young thugs or converse with Martin Luther King, Jr., or Malcolm X with equal confidence and control. Angelou retains a bit of her former naïveté—it takes a couple of years before she finally admits that her husband is not for her—and she remains touchingly down-to-earth as she describes her search for a husband. In these ways, her growth toward self-fulfillment and self-understanding is given compelling reality.

Resources

A wealth of information on Maya Angelou exists on line, on video, and on audiocassette. Some sources of interest for students of Maya Angelou include the following:

Intimate Portrait: Maya Angelou. This videocassette, made in 1996, contains an overview of Angelou's life and career, beginning with her childhood. Her brother and son are interviewed, along with Angelou herself. Oprah Winfrey narrates.

Maya Angelou Links and Resources. This Web site features biographical information, a selection of her works, interviews, and links. This site was a *Los Angeles Times* pick for excellent on-line resources. (http://ucaswww.mcm.uc.edu/worldfest/about.html)

Black Pearls: The Poetry of Maya Angelou. On this 1998 compact disc from Atlantic/Rhino Records, Angelou reads thirty-eight poems from her early career. It is also available on audiocassette.

Videos. *Maya Angelou: Portrait of Greatness* (1993) records Angelou on a visit to Stamps, Arkansas. In *Maya Angelou: Perspective* (1996), Angelou speaks about the healing power of teachers and poetry, reads from her works, and shares personal stories. *An Evening with Maya Angelou* (1999) is a seventy-three-minute tape of Angelou lecturing at Western Washington University.

BERNARD E. MORRIS

Margaret Atwood

BORN: November 18, 1939, Ottawa, Canada
IDENTIFICATION: Late twentieth-century Canadian writer noted for her feminist fiction centering on mythic themes, as well as her poetry and literary criticism.

Margaret Atwood is best known for her fiction, particularly her novels. After her first novel, *The Edible Woman* (1969), her fiction received steadily increasing amounts of critical attention. Novels such as *Surfacing* (1972), *The Handmaid's Tale* (1985), *Cat's Eye* (1988), and *The Robber Bride* (1993) represent characteristic themes of women learning to deal with a world in which men hold most of the power. Her Canadian settings are also significant, for Atwood has been an active promoter of Canadian literature. In addition to her novels and short stories, she has written critical essays on Canadian literature. She is among the most versatile of North American writers, and she has published a substantial body of poetry, in addition to her fiction and criticism.

The Writer's Life

Margaret Eleanor Atwood was born in Ottawa, Ontario, on November 18, 1939, the second of three children. Her parents, Carl and Margaret Killam Atwood, had roots in Nova Scotia, and Atwood's father, an entomologist, took his family with him into the northern Quebec wilderness where he spent part of each year in field research. Atwood offers fictional versions of the experience in several works, most especially in her novel *Cat's Eye*. The family continued to spend summers in the wilderness even after they settled in Toronto in 1946.

The Future Writer. In Toronto, Atwood attended public schools and felt an early urge to write. She joked that she went through a "dark period" between the ages of eight and sixteen when she quit writing, but in high school, influenced by Edgar Allen Poe, she decided that writing would be her life. In the 1950s Canada offered little encouragement to writers, especially to women. The country largely ignored its own scanty literature, and school curricula indicated that only British literature was worth studying. Even American literature made a poor

The Skeena River in British Columbia. The sprawling Canadian wilderness is a recurring image in Atwood's work.

second. As Atwood surveyed writers who might serve as models, she concluded that all of the significant writers were male. Female writers—especially female novelists of the nineteenth century—seemed mostly to have had short, unhappy lives. Certainly they had sacrificed marriage and families for their art.

Atwood committed herself to art, reluctantly concluding that she, too, might be forced to sacrifice the comforts of family. At about the same time, she read Robert Graves's portrait of the creative female in *The White Goddess: A Historical Grammar of Poetic Myth* (1948), whom he defined as an artist inspired by the force that both creates and destroys.

University Student.
Atwood graduated from Toronto's Leaside High School in 1957 and entered the honors program at Victoria College of the University of Toronto. There she studied under Northrup Frye, whose examination of mythic themes in literature was an important influence on Atwood's writing. Frye introduced her to the works of the eighteenth-century English poet and engraver William Blake. Blake's poetry is characterized by his intense private mythology, through which he attempted to resolve a world of opposing forces, most particularly humankind's desires for pleasure and expression. These desires, Blake believed, are thwarted by repressive institutions that humans themselves have created. These themes have been important in Atwood's own work.

During her undergraduate years, Atwood wrote for her college literary magazine. She graduated in 1961 and her first volume of poetry, *Double Persephone,* was published in the same year. The next year she received a master's degree from Radcliffe College in Massachusetts, where she studied the nineteenth-century novel. After winning a Woodrow Wilson fellowship, she con-tinued her studies at Harvard University, concentrating on Victorian literature and the gothic romance. The latter subject figures largely in her novel *Lady Oracle* (1976), as does the series of stopgap jobs she held during this time.

During her work at Harvard, Atwood studied under Perry Miller, a scholar of early American literature. Miller specialized in Puritan literature, a subject interesting to Atwood because of her own Puritan ancestors. It also suggested to her that Canadians should give greater attention to their own early literature, which was, she felt certain, as significant as Puritan sermons.

A Life in Art.
Atwood's post-Harvard years were busy ones. During this period, she got married and held a variety of jobs teaching English in Canadian universities. In 1964 she worked with artist Charles Pachter, who hand-printed some of her early poems. Also at this time, Atwood was moved to reexamine the life

Artist Charles Pachter made his close friend the subject of this 1980 portrait, *Margaret Atwood with Mug.*

Atwood in a photograph taken on her farm near Alliston, Ontario, where she spent many productive and peaceful years before moving back to Toronto.

of Susanna Moodie, an early Canadian immigrant whose work Atwood had first encountered in the sixth grade. Atwood felt drawn to Moodie and created a long sequence of poems about her. These were eventually published in 1970 as *The Journals of Susanna Moodie*, a testament to Atwood's belief in the significance of the Canadian experience.

Atwood's flourishing writing career joined with her social and political interests to make the late 1960s and early 1970s a time of high visibility and some controversy for her. Her feminism provided readers with one focus for controversy, and her nationalism offered another. She has staunchly supported Canadian literature, but at the same time she has argued that there is a tendency on the part of Canada's authors to portray Canada's people and landscapes as victims of the forces of nature and exploitation. This theme is also linked with Atwood's view that women are often victims and, like Canada itself, often participate in their own victimization. Neither

view has been universally popular with the people it describes.

In addition to her novels and poems, Atwood has published many magazine articles. She has written two television scripts for the CBC, *The Servant Girl* (1974) and *Snowbird* (1981), as well as an early choral composition for radio, *The Trumpets of Summer* (1964), for the music of John Beckwith.

Maturity. In 1973 Atwood divorced her first husband and left teaching and her editorial position at the House of Anansi Press to move to a farm near Alliston, Ontario, with novelist Graeme Gibson. The move marked a new direction for her. Within three years, she gave birth to a daughter, Jess, and evidently found the domestic life that she had feared her art would deny her. Although Atwood and Gibson eventually left the farm to return to Toronto, Atwood noted the pleasure she and Gibson had taken in gardening and in doing the other ordinary things connected with family life, such as attending their daughter's school visitation nights.

Domestic tranquility did not reduce Atwood's productivity or popularity. *The Handmaid's Tale* painted a dark picture of a nation run by religious fundamentalists and fostered many discussions about the connections between religion, politics, and feminism. To many feminists, the novel was a timely response to several religious groups' well-publicized positions on women's roles in the church and public life. It seemed that the Handmaids' world was just around the corner.

Alias Grace (1996) raised similar issues in a more veiled way. It was based on the true story of two murders in nineteenth-century Ontario and on Grace Marks, the woman who was sentenced to a mental hospital for the killings. It raised questions about whether Marks was a murderer or the victim of a man she had trusted.

Although Atwood has never relished great media attention about her private life, she has often been willing to talk about her work. As one of Canada's most productive and versatile writers, she has continued to be important as a literary personality, as well as a novelist and poet.

HIGHLIGHTS IN ATWOOD'S LIFE

1939   Margaret Eleanor Atwood is born on November 18 in Ottawa, Canada.

1946   Family moves to Toronto.

1961   Atwood receives bachelor's degree in English language and literature from Victoria College, University of Toronto; wins E. J. Pratt medal for *Double Persephone*, her first published book of poems.

1962   Receives master's degree from Radcliffe College.

1962–1963 Studies Victorian literature and gothic romance at Harvard University.

1964–1965 Lectures in English literature, University of British Columbia, Vancouver.

1964   Begins collaboration with artist friend Charles Pachter, who prints her early poems in limited editions.

1965–1967 Studies American literature at Harvard.

1966   Wins Governor-General's Literary Award for *The Circle Game*.

1968–1969 Teaches creative writing at the University of Alberta.

1969   Publishes first novel, *The Edible Woman*.

1971–1972 Teaches English literature at York University in Toronto.

1972   Publishes the controversial *Survival: A Thematic Guide to Canadian Literature*.

1971–1973 Editor and member of board of directors for House of Anansi Press during a period of political activism.

1972–1973 Writer-in-residence at University of Toronto.

1973   Leaves teaching and resigns from House of Anansi; divorces first husband and moves to a farm in Ontario with novelist Graeme Gibson to support herself by writing.

1974   Begins to publish short stories.

1976   Publishes *Lady Oracle*; daughter Jess is born.

1980   Sherrill Grace's *Violent Duality*, the first book of criticism about Atwood, is published.

1985   Atwood publishes *The Handmaid's Tale*; wins Governor-General's Literary Award.

2000   Wins the Booker Prize, Britain's top Fiction award, for *The Blind Assassin*.

The Writer's Work

Margaret Atwood is known primarily as a novelist and poet. Her work deals mainly with contemporary women and women's issues. Her views typically have been described as feminist. At the same time, her best work has a mythic quality that lifts it well above the level of social realism. Additionally, Atwood has drawn a powerful symbolism from Canada's vast wilderness, where nature seems to work without interference from human efforts to order and contain it. Finally, much of Atwood's writing demonstrates her sense of humor, at once sly and satiric, even when it is directed against herself.

Issues in Atwood's Fiction.

The decades following World War II brought women a growing awareness of a need for power over their lives. Perhaps because of their experience at work while many men were fighting in the war, postwar women of the 1950s and 1960s began to seek the power represented by employment and paychecks. Additionally, they began to assert their equality and their desire to be treated as men's intellectual equals. They expressed increasing resentment at the old social order that had treated women's careers as unimportant and their social significance as secondary to men's, and that had submitted them to a variety of double standards. The most galling of those was the sexual standard that permitted (without necessarily applauding) wide sexual experience for men while insisting that for women the only legitimate sexual experience was within marriage.

The women of Atwood's fiction often find themselves trying to cope with the conflicts arising from this social background. They are realistic characters—wives and mothers, women with jobs or careers—who must cope with contradictory demands. On one hand, the old social order, often in the voice of husbands or parents, urges such women to fit themselves into Canada's repressively middle-class society, to discount their need for self-expression, and

Atwood places high value on the support women lend each other. *Friends*, a 1923 painting by Jan Zrzavy, reflects the comfort often found in companionship.

to suppress any impulse toward self-analysis. On the other hand, their own intellects and spirits pull them toward empowerment through creativity, study, and self-direction in matters of sex and money. Complicating this picture is Atwood's sense that women often invite, and even participate in, their own subjugation. Female complicity is a common theme in Atwood's work. Resolving these conflicts does not necessarily involve relinquishing love, marriage, and child rearing in Atwood's fiction. Her happiest characters find ways of managing these life events, but on their own terms.

In Atwood's fiction, women often find important allies in their friendships both with other women and with men. Friendships with men, however, are often complicated by the possibility of romantic or sexual attraction. Can true friendship exist among people who are not equals? Can men and women be equals in a world that still gives most of the power to men? Atwood's fiction does not say that such friendships are impossible, but that they face many more obstacles than female friendships face.

One result of the women's movement has been the validation of female friendships as sources of support and encouragement for women. Atwood's fiction suggests that women who are able only to value friendships with men, and those who are incapable of making any friends at all, participate in the forces of repression and seriously threaten the social fabric.

Polarities. Duality dominates Atwood's fiction and poetry. An example of this duality is the need for women's self-expression and power balanced against the position society has assigned to women (and their frequent complicity with society's repressive forces).

Images of twins or doubles in Atwood's work help express opposing points of view. Alfred Henry Maurer's *Two Heads* mirrors the dueling forces often found in Atwood's writing.

Another duality rises from Canada itself—the wilderness country in which the prime virtue has been survival. However, in their attempts to survive, humans have done much to tame, confine, and even obliterate that wilderness. Images of twins and doubles, or doppelgängers, are common in Atwood's work.

Atwood's Settings. Atwood frequently sets her fiction in modern Toronto, a large, cosmopolitan city with a subway system, an important university, and a diverse population that includes several large immigrant groups, many from Asia. Although she has protested Toronto's incipient sprawl, Atwood names its streets, shops, hotels, and restaurants in much of her fiction and thus heightens the realistic backdrop against which her characters act.

SOME INSPIRATIONS BEHIND ATWOOD'S WORK

Margaret Atwood's work is richly informed by her early life experiences, some of which are particularly visible as they recur throughout her novels and poems. Atwood's childhood summer encounters with the Canadian wilderness gave her an early insight into the meaning of survival, a theme that she sees at the heart of Canadian literature. The Canadian wilderness also introduced her to the duality of civilization and nature. Her father's entomological research focused her attention on science, which plays a part in some of her fiction.

Atwood has said that her early reading of English poet and essayist Robert Graves's mythological study *The White Goddess* helped to form her early images of a ruinous goddess who destroys her worshippers, an image of victor/victim that has persisted in Atwood's writing.

Atwood's study with scholar and critic Northrup Frye at the University of Toronto introduced her to the work of the eighteenth-century English poet and engraver William Blake, whose powerful private mythology and interest in polarities seem to have influenced Atwood's organization of her own themes. Also during her university days, Atwood began to read Canadian literature, which heightened both her nationalism and her feminism.

Atwood's doctoral studies at Harvard under American literature scholar Perry Miller furthered her interest in the writing of early women, such as seventeenth-century poet Anne Bradstreet, as well as her awareness of Puritan forces on literature and on society.

Atwood's Poetry. Atwood has been a prolific poet, sometimes publishing two poetry volumes a year. Mostly in free verse, her poems often present the themes of her fiction in the sharp relief that naturally results from the compression of poetry. Her poems often deal with relationships between men and women and frequently use metaphoric images of violence to express those relationships. Throughout her career, she has drawn heavily on Greek mythology, transforming its stark and often brutal stories into contemporary commentary. Always ironic, her poems have become increasingly aphoristic, wittily expressing greater truths and principles. While the subject matter of Atwood's work has ranged from Canadian history and love affairs to the craft of writing, her poems commonly share a subtext of reference to women and their concerns in a world that frequently dismisses them.

BIBLIOGRAPHY

Bouson, J. Brooks. *Brutal Choreographies: Oppositional Strategies and Narrative Design in the Novels of Margaret Atwood.* Amherst: University of Massachusetts Press, 1993.

Davey, Frank. *Margaret Atwood: A Feminist Poetics.* Vancouver, B.C.: Talonbooks, 1984.

Deery, June. "Science for Feminists: Margaret Atwood's Body of Knowledge." *Twentieth-Century Literature* 43 (Winter 1997): 470–487.

Goldblatt, Patricia F. "Reconstructing Margaret Atwood's Protagonists." *World Literature Today* 73 (Spring 1999): 275–285.

Jackson, Danita J. "An Interview With Margaret Atwood." *Critique: Studies in Contemporary Fiction* 38 (Winter 1997): 96–105.

McCombs, Judith. *Critical Essays on Margaret Atwood.* Boston: G. K. Hall, 1988.

McCombs, Judith, and Carole Palmer. *Margaret Atwood: A Reference Guide.* Boston: G. K. Hall, 1991.

Sullivan, Rosemary. *The Red Shoes: Margaret Atwood, Starting Out.* Toronto: HarperCollins, 1998.

VanSpanckeren, Kathryn, and Jan Garden Castro, eds. *Margaret Atwood: Vision and Forms.* Carbondale: Southern Illinois University Press, 1988.

Wilson, Sharon Rose. *Margaret Atwood's Fairy-Tale Sexual Politics.* Jackson: University Press of Mississippi, 1993.

ALIAS GRACE

Genre: Novel
Subgenre: Historical mystery
Published: Toronto, 1996
Time period: 1850s
Setting: Ireland; Toronto, Canada

Themes and Issues. This novel is based on the true story of Grace Marks, who was accused of murdering her employer and his housekeeper in the 1850s. Margaret Atwood's attention was first drawn to the case when she worked on *The Journals of Susanna Moodie,* about an immigrant to Canada who recorded her visit to Marks in an insane asylum. Atwood used various records in newspapers and court documents to piece together a version of her story in multiple viewpoints, much as women once pieced together quilts like those used to mark the divisions of this novel.

The Plot. The novel begins when a young American doctor, Simon Jordan, decides to interview convicted murderer Grace Marks in an effort to find out the truth about her crime. Part of the novel is told in letters to and from him, which reveal both his sensitivity and his weakness of character. Throughout the novel a contrast is implied between Grace's simple directness and the flightiness of other women Jordan knows.

Unsure what Jordan wants of her, Grace tells him her story, beginning in Northern Ireland with her family's poverty, her father's alcoholism, and an ever-increasing number of siblings. During the depressed times of the Irish potato famine in the 1840s, Grace sometimes thinks how much easier life would be if an accident killed some of the children.

Immigration to Canada does little to ease the family's circumstances, for Grace's mother dies during the sea journey. In Toronto, as the oldest, Grace is left to manage the household for a father who is increasingly drunk and uninterested in his family's needs. At last she leaves home to go into domestic service, the only work option open to poor young women.

In the course of working for several households, Grace learns how a middle-class home is managed. In one she makes a good friend, her fellow servant Mary Whitney, who treats her kindly. When Mary dies because of a botched abortion, Grace is devastated. Though only sixteen, she leaves her job to work for Mr. Thomas Kinnear in Richmond Hill, a short distance from Toronto.

By the time this photograph was taken in March 1989, Atwood had already established herself as one of the leading Canadian writers of her generation.

LONG FICTION

1969 The Edible Woman
1972 Surfacing
1976 Lady Oracle
1979 Life Before Man
1981 Bodily Harm
1985 The Handmaid's Tale
1988 Cat's Eye
1993 The Robber Bride
1996 Alias Grace
2000 The Blind Assassin

SHORT FICTION

1977 Dancing Girls
1983 Bluebeard's Egg

1983 Murder in the Dark
1991 Wilderness Tips

POETRY

1961 Double Persephone
1964 The Circle Game
1965 Talismans for Children
1965 Kaleidoscopes Baroque: A Poem
1966 Speeches for Dr. Frankenstein
1966 Expeditions
1968 The Animals in That Country
1969 What Was in the Garden

1970 The Journals of Susanna Moodie
1970 Procedures for Underground
1971 Power Politics
1974 You Are Happy
1976 Selected Poems
1978 Two-Headed Poems
1981 True Stories
1983 Snake Poems
1984 Interlunar
1987 Selected Poems II
1991 Poems 1965–1975
1992 Poems 1976–1989
1995 Morning in the Burned House

NONFICTION

1972 Survival: A Thematic Guide to Canadian Literature
1982 Second Words: Selected Critical Prose
1990 Margaret Atwood: Conversations
1992 Good Bones
1996 Strange Things: The Malevolent North in Canadian Literature

CHILDREN'S LITERATURE

1978 Up in the Tree
1980 Anna's Pet (with Joyce Barkhouse)
1995 Princess Prunella and the Purple Peanut (with Maryann Kowalski)

EDITED TEXT

1982 The Oxford Book of Canadian Verse in English

SCREEN PLAYS

1974 The Servant Girl (TV)
1981 Snowbird (TV; with Peter Pearson)

MURDER IN THE DARK
SHORT FICTIONS AND PROSE POEMS
Margaret Atwood

Kinnear is single; the other members of his household are a stableman, James McDermott, and Kinnear's housekeeper/lover, Nancy Montgomery. Grace is oblivious of this relationship, however, and settles happily into her new duties. Only Jeremiah the peddler recognizes Grace from her earlier life. As Grace becomes aware of the relationship between Kinnear and Nancy, their friendship cools, although the news that Nancy is pregnant brings her friend Mary to Grace's mind. During all her conversations with Dr. Jordan, Grace is amazed at his masculine ignorance of the dirty details of managing a house.

The time of the actual murder is nightmarish in Grace's memory. She no longer knows what really happened; consequently, the reader is never sure whether McDermott killed the pair alone, whether Grace helped him, or whether something entirely different happened. Grace flees the house with McDermott, but they are soon apprehended, taken into custody, and finally tried; Grace is found guilty.

Dr. Jordan is eager to find the truth at the bottom of the conflicting reports about Grace. He visits the Kinnear home, and he participates in an effort to hypnotize Grace, but the results are inconclusive. At this point Jordan is called home to the United States to attend to his mother's health. Once there, he abandons his Canadian connections altogether, including his relationship with Grace. Some years later, Grace is pardoned and marries an old friend, allowing her at last to experience a quiet happiness.

Analysis. In an afterword to the novel, Margaret Atwood points out that the contemporary press often treated Grace as a temptress reminiscent of the Greek goddess Circe, a common view of women that Atwood has often discussed. In the novel, however, the reader sees Grace in positive contrast with the upper-class women around her. She also contrasts with Dr. Jordan, a man who seems incapable of recognizing his deepening relationship with Grace or of understanding himself or anyone else. Throughout the novel, Grace demonstrates a clear-headedness and realism that seem to be good omens for her impending marriage.

SOURCES FOR FURTHER STUDY

Meindl, Dieter. "Gender and Narrative Perspective in Margaret Atwood's Stories." In *Margaret Atwood: Writing and Subjectivity* edited by Colin Nicholson. New York: St. Martin's Press, 1994.

Mujica, Barbara. Review of *Alias Grace,* by Margaret Atwood. *Americas* 49 (November/December 1997): 61–73.

Turbide, Diane. "Amazing Atwood." *Maclean's* 109 (September 23, 1996): 42–46.

THE HANDMAID'S TALE
   Genre: Novel
   Subgenre: Dystopian fantasy
   Published: Toronto, 1985
   Time period: The near future
   Setting: Gilead, formerly Cambridge, Massachusetts

Themes and Issues. In writing this dystopian, or anti-utopian, look at a fearful and dehumanized future society, Atwood challenged herself to include only events that had, in some measure, already occurred somewhere in the contemporary world. The result portrays a grim future in which suppression of women has reached a point at which most of them are valued only for their ability to breed. Atwood takes pains to work out some details of the history, politics, and language of the world she creates.

The Plot. The story is told by Offred, a Handmaid in service to a Commander in the postwar world of Gilead. Religious fundamentalists have won in a war against the United States, and women are now in the lowly status assigned to them by a narrow reading of the Bible. Nuclear weapons used during the war have left many women (and men, presumably, although it is illegal to say so) incapable of conceiving children. Those women who are still fertile have been made Handmaids. Assigned to the homes of the upper echelon of rulers, their task is to bear healthy children, whom the rulers' sterile Wives will raise as their own. Handmaids, Wives, and Marthas (servants) are the only significant positions left for women in the new order.

Atwood's feminist concerns inform not only her writing but her artwork as well. Her 1969 watercolor *Lady and Sinister Figure* is part of a collection at the Thomas Fisher Rare Book Library at the University of Toronto.

Atwood 1970

Atwood's 1970 watercolor of a skeleton bride points to the role women often play in their own victimization. The artwork, titled *Death as a Bride*, is housed in the Thomas Fisher Rare Book Library at the University of Toronto.

The Handmaids take on the name of the Commander to whose household they have been assigned (their names begin with *Of-* to designate them as the men's property). They are stripped of all personal freedoms and are not allowed to read, write, or handle money. They are not allowed to wear clothes other than assigned uniforms. Everything has been forbidden while they wait to become pregnant. The term *Handmaid* has been adopted from the story in Genesis 30:1–3 in which childless Rachel asks her husband to impregnate her servant so that she can claim the child.

Offred detests her confinement in a comfortless world. She hates the Commander's hypocritical wife, Serena Joy, and she recalls with passionate longing her life with her husband and daughter before the war. In the days just before the fundamentalists' complete takeover, she recalls, there were signs of events to come. Some women were involved in book burnings and the closings of theaters that showed pornography. Then, women were suddenly stripped of their credit cards and their right to own property. Offred and her husband and daughter made a desperate flight to Canada, but Offred was captured and trained as a Handmaid. She hopes her husband and daughter have escaped.

Offred's Commander has offered her several illicit kindnesses. Knowing how she misses the written word, he has brought her magazines. They even spend some secret evenings playing the word game Scrabble. Offred is grateful for these distractions; her world is grindingly boring. The only legal entertainments for Handmaids are births (which are celebrated mightily by both Handmaids and Wives) and salvagings—revivals combined with political executions.

Offred suspects that an underground resistance movement exists that might bring her news of her daughter, but she also knows that Gilead is networked with a spy system that will punish all

rebels. Still, she attempts to make connections with fellow rebels and even accompanies the Commander to an underground nightclub. There she meets an old friend, Moira, who resisted the Handmaids' training and eventually disappeared. Evidently such women are used as prostitute hostesses in such clubs.

As her time limit for breeding runs out, Offred agrees to have sex with the Commander's chauffeur, an attractive young man who may be a link to the resistance. At Offred's last report, she is climbing into a van that may take her to freedom—or to death. The novel ends with notes from a Canadian conference in the distant

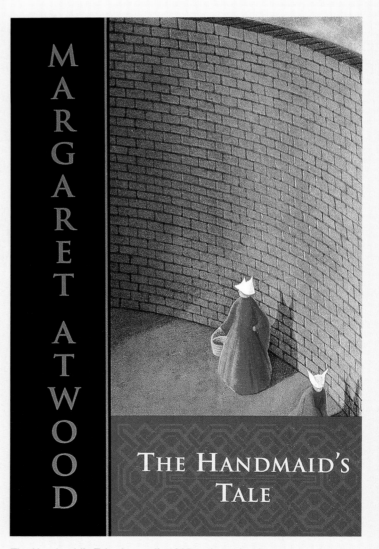

The Handmaid's Tale, Atwood's 1985 anti-utopian fantasy, has been printed many times. This cover adorned the 1998 edition published by Anchor Books.

future, where academics are examining Offred's secretly tape-recorded history.

Analysis. Like most dystopian fiction, *The Handmaid's Tale* offers its readers a satiric view of the world as it might become if it persists in its folly. As such, it has darkly comic elements, particularly in Gilead's linguistic games (*salvagings,* for instance, that are really savagings) as well as in Offred's own ironic voice. As is often the case in Atwood's fiction, women participate in their own suppression, but in Gilead they must risk their lives to escape. Whether escape is even possible is a question the novel leaves unanswered.

SOURCES FOR FURTHER STUDY

Bouson, J. Brooks. "The Misogyny of Patriarchal Culture in *The Handmaid's Tale.*" In *Brutal Choreographies: Oppositional Strategies and Narrative Design in the Novels of Margaret Atwood.* Amherst: University of Massachusetts Press, 1993.

Davidson, Arnold E. "Future Tense: Making History in *The Handmaid's Tale.*" In *Margaret Atwood: Visions and Forms,* edited by Kathryn VanSpanckeren and Jan Garden Castro. Carbondale: Southern Illinois University Press, 1988.

Freibert, Lucy M. "Control and Creativity: The Politics of Risk in Margaret Atwood's *The Handmaid's Tale.*" In *Critical Essays on Margaret Atwood,* edited by Judith McCombs. Boston: G. K. Hall, 1988.

Rubenstein, Roberta. "Nature and Nurture in Dystopia." In *Margaret Atwood: Visions and Forms,* edited by Kathryn VanSpanckeren and Jan Garden Castro. Carbondale: Southern Illinois University Press, 1988.

LADY ORACLE

Genre: Novel
Subgenre: Comic romance
Published: Toronto, 1976
Time period: 1970s
Settings: Terremoto, Italy; London, England; Toronto, Canada

Themes and Issues. *Lady Oracle* offers readers a comic view of some of Atwood's most serious themes. It portrays women in a double view, as heroines in gothic romance and as real

Atwood herself is the artist behind this collage creation, *Moodie and the Wilderness,* which appeared in Atwood's *The Journals of Susanna Moodie* in 1970.

women fighting for validity in a world that tries to fit them to a preconceived pattern. The novel's Joan Foster becomes the central figure of the romance she is writing while she flees her own unhappy marriage. Atwood has called this the most heavily rewritten of her novels. In rewriting, she changed Joan's long narrative letter to Arthur into an address to a hospitalized reporter.

The Plot. In Italy, Joan Foster is evidently on the run, but only through her self-revealing monologue that constitutes the novel does the reader understand what has happened. Early on, however, she discloses that she is a writer of gothic romances, "bodice rippers," in which innocent women are threatened—often sexually—by attractive but dangerous men, whom they try to seduce into marriage without sacrificing themselves to their lovers' passions or violence. Her husband, Arthur, has never learned that Joan writes such novels.

When Joan was growing up, her mother disliked her because she was fat, thus contradicting her mother's romantic notions of how women should be. Among many unhappy childhood moments, the most painful for Joan was being denied the butterfly role in a children's dance recital. The image of an elephantine fat lady in a tutu balancing on a tightrope dominates Joan's imagination still.

Joan's unconventional Aunt Lou was her only childhood friend, a woman with a kind heart and a sense of style whose will inspired Joan to lose weight and leave home for London. There she moves in with Paul, a Polish count, the dangerous sort of man she will later write about. Paul makes part of his living by writing romances under the name of Mavis Quilp. Joan quickly learns the trade herself. Through the rest of *Lady Oracle,* she includes snippets of her current project in her tale.

Fearful of Paul's jealousy, Joan leaves him for Arthur, an ineffectual young man she has met while he demonstrates at Speaker's Corner at Hyde Park in London. Arthur's leftist politics reject the bourgeois convention of marriage, but he allows Joan to move in with him. When Joan returns to Canada after her mother's death, Arthur follows her and at last marries her, mostly in order to save money on his rent. Moreover, Toronto is too puritanical to put up with unmarried cohabitation.

Joan continues to write secretly while she keeps house for Arthur, but then she stumbles into success. Using a sort of automatic writing, Joan writes a romance that breaks the stereotyped patterns such novels usually follow, and she suddenly becomes a media star. Arthur resents her changed fortune and becomes increasingly distant. Joan has a romantic fling with an avant-garde artist, the Royal Porcupine, but at last, despairing, she fakes her own death and goes back to Italy, where she hopes Arthur will join her. Instead, she is discovered by a reporter who had uncovered her affair with the Royal Porcupine. As the novel ends, Joan is waiting for the reporter to reveal her secret. She thinks he may be the only man who really knows anything about her.

Analysis. *Lady Oracle* is a comic novel in which Atwood laughs at some of her own themes and emblems. For instance, Joan sends her novel to the Black Widow Press, another name for Anansi, Atwood's own House of Anansi Press. Atwood also burlesques the conventions of the gothic romance. The bits of Joan's novel reveal the increasingly outrageous actions of her characters, who threaten to break loose from the strict roles assigned them by the genre. On a more serious level, Joan does exactly what her characters are doing—she refuses the role into which her mother (and, by extension, the rest of society) have tried to fit her. She has had a hand in her own misery, having spent much of her adulthood trying to please Paul and Arthur. When she hits the reporter, who has cracked her disguise, with a wine bottle, she seems to have broken out of all her disguises and into a new level of her life.

SOURCES FOR FURTHER STUDY

Bouson, J. Brooks. "Comic Storytelling as Escape and Narcissistic Self-Expression in Atwood's *Lady Oracle.*" In *The Empathetic Reader: A Study of the Narcissistic Character and the Drama of the Self.* Amherst: University of Massachusetts Press, 1989.

Fee, Margery. *The Fat Lady Dances: Margaret Atwood's "Lady Oracle."* Toronto: ECW Press, 1993.

McMillan, Ann. "The Transforming Eye: *Lady Oracle* and the Gothic Tradition." In *Margaret Atwood: Vision and Forms,* edited by Kathryn VanSpanckeren and Jan Garden Castro. Carbondale: Southern Illinois University Press, 1988.

Rao, Eleanora. "Margaret Atwood's *Lady Oracle:* Writing Against Notions of Unity." In *Margaret Atwood: Writing and Subjectivity,* edited by Colin Nicholson. New York: St. Martin's Press, 1994.

Other Works

CAT'S EYE (1988). This book traces the career of its narrator, the successful painter Elaine Risley, who has returned to Toronto to help a local gallery arrange a retrospective show of her work. Her return to Toronto wakens vivid childhood memories of her family's move from the wilderness to a raw housing development in postwar Toronto and especially of her childhood friends there. One of them was Grace Smeath, from a sanctimonious household that represents the most repressive attitudes of the middle class. Grace's mother becomes an icon of that period for Elaine; she has been the subject of many of Elaine's pictures.

Another friend was the self-willed and dangerous Cordelia, the only one of her friends Elaine thinks might turn up at the gallery. Her childhood calls up wrenching memories for Elaine; her friends allied themselves against her for months, making her life a hell until finally they abandoned her in a dangerous snow-filled ravine where she nearly drowned. Only in high school did Elaine learn to take control of their relationship.

Now Elaine copes with the memories of her first marriage (she is staying in her ex-husband's studio), with an unexpected protest against her pictures by religious fundamentalists (rather like Grace Smeath's mother), and especially with memories of Cordelia, whose early talents were lost to mental illness. At last she exorcises Cordelia's ghost on a long walk through their old neighborhood, regretting the loss of a friendship that never was.

THE JOURNALS OF SUSANNA MOODIE (1970). This long poem was inspired by the journals of a real woman who emigrated from England to Canada in the 1830s. Atwood first became aware of Moodie in her grade school

This cover adorned an edition published by Oxford University Press in the late 1990s.

studies, when she considered Moodie dull. However, in adulthood Atwood felt compelled by the triple themes of womanhood, wilderness, and early literature present in Moodie's journals.

Margaret Atwood presents Moodie's journals poetically, portraying three time periods: 1832–1840, 1840–1871, and 1871–1969, with the latter being the time when Atwood was writing the poems. Individual poems within each section represent events in Moodie's life: fires, the death of her children, an episode of racial violence. As a group, however, the poems constitute an examination of the paradox of the settler who is both conqueror of the wilderness and victim of it, who loves and hates it at the same time.

In poems from the first section, Moodie records how unprepared she was for wilderness life; she doesn't know how to bake bread or use a washtub. The real wilderness, she says, is the immigrants' own ignorance. After she has endured both a forest fire and a house fire, she concludes that no place in the wilderness is safe.

In the second section, Moodie's young son drowns, and she notes that his death gives her a special tie to her new country: "I planted him in this country like a flag." In another poem, referring to the immense power of wilderness, she says that "anything planted here would come up blood."

Poems in the third section extend into the twentieth century, beyond Moodie's death, as

Ilya Mashkov's painting *Bread* (Russian State Museum, Saint Petersburg) focuses the observer's attention on a common and symbolic substance, as Atwood does in her written work "Bread," which is part of her collection *Murder in the Dark*.

she tells modern inhabitants of Toronto about the duality of life that requires both civilizing forces of humans and the brutal power of the wild. Still, she says, "at the last judgement we will all be trees."

MURDER IN THE DARK (1983). This collection of short fictions and prose poems, as the subtitle calls them, makes a good introduction to the witty and aphoristic quality of much of Atwood's poetry. To some degree, they all play mind games with their reader, but they have more serious themes as well.

"Happy Endings" pretends to be a set of instructions for writing a certain kind of fiction, the sort that is sometimes called women's fiction because of its domestic settings and romantic themes. Atwood sets up an initial situation in which "John and Mary meet." The novelist/reader is to decide what happens next, and Atwood offers various possibilities, most of which end disastrously. At last Atwood concludes that it is the beginnings of fiction that are fun.

"Bread" performs similar transformations. Atwood begins by describing a piece of bread, covered perhaps with peanut butter and honey. She describes people's careless attitude toward bread. She then offers other scenarios—a famine in which children are dying for bread, or a starving sibling—to frame her final question about bread created by fiction: "Can you eat it?"

THE ROBBER BRIDE (1993). This novel chronicles the long history of three middle-aged friends, Tony, Charis, and Roz, each of whom has been wounded by a fourth woman, Zenia, the "robber bride" of the title. When the story opens, the three are lunching in a restaurant when they are astonished to see Zenia enter; they had attended her funeral only the year before. In the alternating sections that follow, the reader learns how Zenia has stolen money, men, and self-respect from each of them.

Tony, a military historian with a talent for speaking backward, grew up with a distant mother who abandoned the family; Tony's father drank himself to death. Affection-starved Tony was thrilled to fall in love with West during their college days, and devastated when he left her for Zenia, though he later returned. Zenia also took Charis's Billy, an American draft dodger whom Zenia turned in to the Royal Canadian Mounted Police, leaving pregnant Charis alone with only her mystic powers. Some years later she also lured away businesswoman Roz's husband. In each case, she coupled her theft with words so brutal they could not be ignored.

Now Zenia seems to have returned to start again on Roz's grown son Larry. The three friends enter a plot to confront, possibly even to kill, Zenia, but circumstances (or perhaps Charis's "other self," the ghost of the sexually abused child she once was) dispose of Zenia for them. They are left as victorious survivors. For all the fickle men in *The Robber Bride,* three turn out to be good and faithful, even West.

Resources

After 1970, Margaret Atwood contributed her papers, holographs (handwritten papers), and manuscripts, as well as unpublished works, to the Thomas Fisher Rare Book Library at the University of Toronto. Other resources include:

The Margaret Atwood Society. This academic society maintains a valuable Web site with information about its meetings and other activities. It also lists an exhaustive bibliography of Atwood's published works, including sound recordings and artwork, and it furnishes links to additional Atwood sites, as well as to other sites connected with Canadian literature. (http://www.cariboo.bc.ca/atwood)

The Margaret Atwood Information Web Site. This official Margaret Atwood site is maintained by the author herself. It contains a detailed chronology of the author's life, essays on writing, lists of books by and about Margaret Atwood, as well as links to other Atwood sites, including a bibliography of research sources. (http://www.web.net/owtoad)

The *Salon* Interview. In January of 1997, Atwood gave an interview with Laura Miller in the on-line magazine *Salon,* in which she discusses the writing of her novel *Alias Grace.*
(http://www.salonmagazine.com/jan97/ interview970120.html).

***The Book Show* Interview.** A transcript of Atwood's 1994 lengthy interview on *The Book Show,* in which she discusses *The Robber Bride,* can be seen at the Writers Online site.
(http://www.albany.edu/writers-inst/atwood.html).

Study Guide to Margaret Atwood: *The Handmaid's Tale.* A detailed study guide to the novel, with chapter-by-chapter reading notes, is accessible on line. (http://www.wsu.edu:8000/~brians/science_fiction/ handmaid.html).

ANN D. GARBETT

James Baldwin

BORN: August 2, 1924, New York, New York
DIED: December 1, 1987, St. Paul-de-Vence, France
IDENTIFICATION: Prolific African American writer of essays, novels, short stories, and plays during the second half of the twentieth century. Best known for his examinations of family, religion, sexual preference, and racial tensions.

James Baldwin was a major force in twentieth-century literature, both as a literary stylist and as an advocate of social justice. Along with Martin Luther King, Jr., Malcolm X, and Medgar Evers, Baldwin stands as one of the great voices for progress in racial relations and the search for a black identity in American culture. His work continually describes the great price and power of love among all humankind.

The Writer's Life

On August 2, 1924, Emma Berdis Jones gave birth to James Arthur Jones in Harlem, New York City. In 1927 she married David Baldwin, a Baptist preacher in Harlem, and her son took his stepfather's name, becoming James Arthur Baldwin. James never knew his biological father. His stepfather—who came to the marriage with his own twelve-year-old son, Samuel, and his mother, Barbara Ann Baldwin, a former slave—remained married to Emma until he died in 1943. The marriage produced eight additional children, three boys and five girls.

To support his family, David Baldwin worked as a common laborer. His earnings were not sufficient, however, and the family was forced to move often and, on occasion, to depend on public aid. After a fight with his father, Samuel left the family, and James, now the oldest child, helped his mother raise the other children.

Childhood. James's stepfather was a disciplinarian, and he controlled James's activities, filling his life with fear. James's mother, however, counterbalanced her husband, as she advocated patience and loving acceptance of others.

In 1929 James Baldwin began his schooling at New York City's Public School 24. His intellectual potential was recognized by the school principal, Gertrude E. Ayer, who referred him to Orilla Miller, a Works Progress Administration (WPA) Theater Project worker in the public schools. Orilla Miller also recognized Baldwin's intellectual promise and took him to see plays and movies. In the attic of the school building, she helped mount a production of his first play. Both Miller and Baldwin admired Charles Dickens, and Baldwin developed an interest in Dickens's novel *A Tale of Two Cities* (1859).

In September 1935, Baldwin entered Frederick Douglass Junior High

Baldwin sprawls across his bed to jot down some notes in his New York City apartment in January 1963. He found this writing position comfortable.

Edward Burra's 1934 painting *Harlem* (Tate Gallery, London) depicts a social life that Baldwin would have been familiar with as a child growing up in Harlem.

HIGHLIGHTS IN BALDWIN'S LIFE

1924	James Baldwin is born James Arthur Jones on August 2 in Harlem, New York.
1927	Changes name to James Arthur Baldwin when his mother marries David Baldwin.
1929	Begins schooling at P.S. 24; meets Orilla Miller, who encourages his interest in the theater.
1938	Enters De Witt Clinton High School and coedits *The Magpie*.
1938–1940	Preaches in a Pentecostal church in Harlem.
1940	Leaves home and church on the same day.
1948	Moves to Paris.
1954	Wins Guggenheim Fellowship.
1956	Receives National Institute of Arts and Letters Award and *Partisan Review* Fellowship.
1957	Investigates racism in the South.
1959	Receives Ford Foundation grant.
1961	Visits Israel and Turkey.
1962	Publishes *Another Country*; travels to Africa with his sister Gloria.
1963	Publishes *The Fire Next Time*; becomes active in the Civil Rights movement.
1964	*Blues for Mister Charlie* opens on Broadway.
1965	*The Amen Corner* opens on Broadway.
1968	Baldwin is criticized in Eldridge Cleaver's *Soul on Ice*; attends the funeral of Martin Luther King, Jr.
1970–1971	Battles health problems, including hepatitis; buys home in St. Paul-de-Vence, France.
1978	Teaches at Bowling Green College in Ohio; awarded Martin Luther King, Jr., Memorial Medal.
1979–1980	Teaches at the University of California, Berkeley.
1981	Researches Atlanta child murders.
1983–1984	Teaches at the University of Massachusetts in Amherst; is hospitalized for exhaustion.
1986	Made Officer of the Legion of Honor in France.
1987	Dies on December 1 in Saint Paul-de-Vence, France.

School. Countée Cullen, a leading poet of the Harlem Renaissance, was Baldwin's teacher and the advisor to the school's literary club. Baldwin became one of the editors of *The Douglass Pilot* and contributed poems, essays, and stories. He also expanded his reading, showing interest in Harriet Beecher Stowe's novel *Uncle Tom's Cabin* (1852) and researching the history of Harlem for an essay titled "Harlem Then and Now."

In September 1938, Baldwin entered New York City's De Witt Clinton High School. With friends, he edited *The Magpie*, the school's literary magazine. For this publication, he wrote several stories and an interview with poet Countée Cullen. He struggled in some of his academic subjects but maintained strong performances in English and history. He received his high school diploma in January 1942.

During his years in junior high school, Baldwin attended various Pentecostal churches. He experienced a religious revelation and became a youthful minister at Fireside Pentecostal Assembly, where he preached regularly for three years. Baldwin's outlook subsequently began to range beyond the church, however, and he eventually left his ministry.

Starting a Literary Career.

After short-lived jobs at an army depot, a meat-packing plant, and a restaurant, Baldwin focused on writing and moved to Greenwich Village to pursue the life of a writer. He emerged as a regular reviewer for *The Nation*, *The New Leader*, and *Commentary*. In 1948 his story "Previous Condition" and his essay "The Harlem Ghetto" were published in *Commentary*.

In November 1948, Baldwin moved to Paris, France. There he met fellow African American writer Richard Wright, who had moved to France the previous year. Living in an inexpensive hotel, Baldwin gained access to a diverse intellectual community in Paris and made many friends. His reading encompassed French, Russian, and American literature, and he gave detailed study to the works of Anglo-American writer Henry James.

Baldwin continued to write essays, and in 1949 "Everybody's Protest Novel" appeared in *Partisan Review*. This essay mounted an attack on *Uncle Tom's Cabin* and criticized Wright's novel *Native Son* (1940), straining his friendship with Wright. Their connection ended in 1951 when Baldwin published "Many Thousands Gone," another attack on Wright, in *Partisan Review*. In the winter of 1951–1952, Baldwin retreated to a chalet in Switzerland owned by the family of his friend Lucien Happersberger. There, he completed *Go Tell It on the Mountain*, which was published in May 1953.

In Greenwich Village, Baldwin had sexual relations with both men and women but favored homosexuality. In Paris, he fell in love with Happersberger. Baldwin's homosexuality eventually became clear, but he was never ostentatious. His novel *Giovanni's Room* (1956) explored the narrator's struggle to find his sexual identity but focused mostly on the broader issue of love. For Baldwin, love always remained more important than the choice between homosexuality and heterosexuality.

Writing Success.

Baldwin continued to publish essays, winning assignments for *Partisan Review*, *Encounter*, *Esquire*, and *Mademoiselle*. In 1961 his second collection of essays, *Nobody Knows My Name: More Notes of a Native Son*, sold more than two million copies. Despite mixed reviews, his novel *Another Country* became a national best-seller and sold four million copies in 1962. In January of 1963, *The Fire Next Time*, another work in the essay form, was published and sold one million copies.

Baldwin's career as a dramatist gained force in 1964 when *Blues for Mister Charlie* opened on Broadway in April. *The Amen Corner*, which had been written in 1954, opened on Broadway a year later and also played in Europe. In 1986 *The Amen Corner* was revived in London and ran for seven months.

A tireless writer, Baldwin published his novel *Tell Me How Long the Train's Been Gone* in 1968. In 1971 his conversations with anthropologist Margaret Mead led to the publication of *A Rap on Race*. In 1972 his essay collection *No Name in the Street* was published, as well as the dramatic work *One Day When I Was Lost: A Scenario Based on "The Autobiography of Malcolm X."* Baldwin returned to the national best-seller list in 1974 with the novel *If Beale Street Could Talk.* After an extended conversation with the poet Nikki Giovanni, he published *A Dialogue* in 1975.

Baldwin's prolific output continued in 1976 with the publication of an extended prose piece on the cinema titled *The Devil Finds Work,* as well as *Little Man, Little Man: A Story of Childhood,* which featured illustrations by Yoran Cazac. In the fall of 1979, Dial published Baldwin's novel *Just Above My Head.* The poetry collection *Jimmy's Blues* was published in

England in 1983 and in the United States in 1984. In 1985 *The Evidence of Things Not Seen,* an expanded version of an essay originally published in *Playboy,* was published by Holt, Rinehart and Winston. *The Price of the Ticket: Collected Nonfiction, 1948–1985* and *James Baldwin: Collected Essays,* published in 1985 and 1998, respectively, gathered together Baldwin's extraordinary output as an essayist. On public television in 1985, a dramatic creation of *Go Tell It on the Mountain* was aired.

Social Activism. In the summer of 1957, Baldwin made his first extended passage in the South, working for *Partisan Review* and *Harper's Magazine.* He gathered information in North Carolina, Georgia, Alabama, and Tennessee. Striving to find connections among people, he met with a vast range of public figures: Malcolm X, Elijah Muhammad, James Meredith, Medgar Evers, Robert F. Kennedy, Jerome Smith, Kenneth Clark, Lorraine Hansberry, Harry Belafonte, Lena Horne, James Forman, Sidney Poitier, Thurgood Marshall, and many others. For an essay published in *Playboy* in 1981, Baldwin investigated a series of murders of black children in Atlanta. He later expanded this essay and published it in book form as *The Evidence of Things Not Seen.* Baldwin's writings always called into question the problems created by the differences among human beings, and Baldwin's works challenged his many readers to pay the price necessary for the victory of love.

Despite his dedication to social justice, Baldwin was sometimes viewed with hostil-

William H. Johnson's painting *Church on Lenox Avenue* (Smithsonian American Art Museum in Washington, D.C.) depicts a place of worship in Harlem. Baldwin considered his three years as a Pentecostal preacher in Harlem a rich source of his writing.

ity. For example, civil rights activist Eldridge Cleaver claimed in his book *Soul on Ice* (1968) that Baldwin was not sufficiently radical. In 1973 Henry Louis Gates, an influential scholar of African American literature, submitted a story on Baldwin to *Time* magazine. His editor refused to print the piece, declaring that Baldwin was "passé."

In 1987, while again living in St. Paul-de-Vence, France, Baldwin submitted to tests that revealed cancer of the esophagus. Surgery provided some relief, but his condition later worsened, and he died on December 1, 1987. A funeral service at the Episcopal Cathedral of St. John the Divine paid homage to one of the century's great literary artists and social activists. The service included eulogies by Toni Morrison, Maya Angelou, and Amiri Baraka.

Baldwin speaking at the Birmingham Bombing Protest (top right) on September 22, 1963, and Baldwin emphasizing his views with his hands (above), date and location unknown.

James Baldwin's greatest writing accomplishments are probably in the essay and the novel. His prose style is either intricate or direct, but the message is always clear. His works dramatize personal and social problems. Instead of supplying compromising solutions, he challenges individuals to discover the ideals that represent the human potential for love.

Issues in Baldwin's Writings. Issues of family, friendship, and love are central in much of Baldwin's writing. His work examines family relationships among fathers, mothers, brothers, sisters, and in-laws. He explores friendship and love, searching for an answer to the question of what it means to be Christian. Baldwin shows both the sincerity and hypocrisy of people in the Pentecostal church.

Another central issue for Baldwin is the problem of choosing safety over commitment to life. Rather than follow the truth in the heart, a character may succumb to fears about consequences. Electing to play it safe often forces characters into desperate, shameful dishonesty. Baldwin often singles out the cruel and shameless, whether they be racist police officers or savagely hypocritical murderers. In many of his works, he asks how America can awaken from the "racial nightmare." In *The Fire Next Time*, Baldwin calls on "the relatively conscious whites and the relatively conscious blacks" to join together to make the world a place where individuals can rise above their racial backgrounds.

One of Baldwin's most frequent themes is that love is not easily affirmed but rather requires strength and commitment. This is the price of being a part of the human family. He suggests that people are too often unready or unwilling to accept the sacrifices, pains, and sorrows accompanying commitment to love. Nevertheless, he maintains, those who are ready to pay the price for love can change the course of history. Those committed to love redeem themselves and give life value and meaning.

Baldwin's Literary Legacy. Baldwin stands as a major figure in twentieth-century literature. His fiction reveals a diversity of style and narrative approach that gives artistic strength to social themes and the affirmation of love. His essays are eloquent and carefully argued, challenging common assumptions. His plays refuse to make compromises with prevail-

This 1946 painting, *Can Fire in the Park* (The Smithsonian American Art Museum, Washington, D.C.), is by artist Beauford Delaney, a lifetime friend of Baldwin's. Delaney encouraged Baldwin to take up writing full-time.

James Baldwin's childhood was greatly influenced by his stepfather's stern discipline and racial views, but later in life he was able to look back with sympathy on his stepfather's struggles with racism and the challenge of feeding and clothing his large family. Baldwin's mother counterbalanced his stepfather's stern demeanor, providing an emphasis on love that inspired the great love Baldwin felt could be kindled in the hearts of all men.

Another key influence in Baldwin's childhood was the government worker Orilla Miller, who worked personally with him, taking him to plays and movies and helping to develop his dramatic interests. Miller invited him to join her family in discussions of social justice, awakening his sense of social activism. Baldwin and Miller both enjoyed the writings of Charles Dickens, and as their friendship endured into Baldwin's adulthood, so did their mutual interest in Dickens and films based on Dickens's work.

Baldwin himself looked back on his three years of Pentecostal preaching as the source of his writing. His work often reflects the cadence and moral themes of sermons. Beauford Delaney, a Greenwich Village artist, helped Baldwin to find the courage to leave the church and dedicate himself to writing. Throughout his life, Baldwin remained loyal to Delaney.

The violent deaths of Medgar Evers, Malcolm X, and Martin Luther King, Jr., during the 1960s stunned Baldwin. To some degree, dealing with these tragedies hampered Baldwin's productivity. Ultimately, however, their deaths became a bitter source of inspiration.

Jacob Lawrence's 1958 oil painting, *Men Exist for the Sake of One Another. Teach Them Then or Bear with Them*, part of the Great Ideas of Western Man series at the Smithsonian American Art Museum in Washington, D.C., depicts the love Baldwin believed could be found in the hearts of all human beings.

ing views or marketing concerns, and as a playwright, Baldwin was ahead of his time. Baldwin's achievement is perhaps best seen in his prolific literary production in diverse forms. Only great writers can write so much in such a range of genres. Despite his achievements Baldwin does have detractors who find that he is out of style or insufficiently aggressive. These views should be acknowledged, but given the perspective of advancing years, most critics now appreciate the breadth of Baldwin's production and the depth of his convictions.

BIBLIOGRAPHY

Bloom, Harold, ed. *James Baldwin*. New York: Chelsea House, 1986.

Campbell, James. *Talking at the Gates: A Life of James Baldwin*. New York: Penguin, 1991.

Leeming, David Adams. *James Baldwin: A Biography*. New York: Holt, 1994.

McBride, Dwight, ed. *James Baldwin Now*. New York: New York University Press, 1999.

Miller, D. Quentin. *Re-Viewing James Baldwin*. Philadelphia: Temple University Press, 2000.

Morrison, Toni, ed. *James Baldwin: Collected Essays*. New York: Library of America, 1998.

Porter, Horace A. *Stealing the Fire: The Arts and Protest of James Baldwin*. Middletown, Conn.: Wesleyan University Press, 1989.

Standley, Fred L., and Louis H. Pratt, eds. *Conversations with James Baldwin*. Jackson: University Press of Mississippi, 1989.

Troupe, Quincy. *James Baldwin: The Legacy*. New York: Simon and Schuster/Touchstone Press, 1989.

Washington, Bryan R. *The Politics of Exile: Ideology in Henry James, F. Scott Fitzgerald, and James Baldwin*. Boston: Northeastern University Press, 1995.

LONG FICTION

1953   Go Tell It on the Mountain
1956   Giovanni's Room
1962   Another Country
1968   Tell Me How Long the Train's Been Gone
1974   If Beale Street Could Talk
1979   Just Above My Head

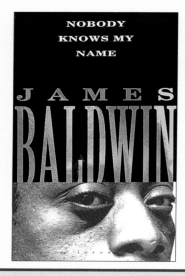

NONFICTION

1955   Notes of a Native Son
1961   Nobody Knows My Name: More Notes of a Native Son
1963   The Fire Next Time
1964   Nothing Personal (with Richard Avedon)
1971   A Rap on Race (with Margaret Mead)
1972   No Name in the Street
1975   A Dialogue (with Nikki Giovanni)
1976   The Devil Finds Work
1985   The Evidence of Things Not Seen
1985   The Price of the Ticket: Collected Nonfiction, 1948–1985
1989   Conversations with James Baldwin, ed. Fred L. Standley and Louis H. Pratt
1998   James Baldwin: Collected Essays, ed. Toni Morrison

SHORT FICTION

1965   Going to Meet the Man

POETRY

1983   Jimmy's Blues: Selected Poems

CHILDREN'S LITERATURE

1976   Little Man, Little Man: A Story of Childhood

PLAYS

1954   The Amen Corner
1964   Blues for Mister Charlie
1972   One Day When I Was Lost: A Scenario Based on "The Autobiography of Malcolm X"

Baldwin the Dramatist

During his childhood, James Baldwin met Orilla Miller, a Works Progress Administration (WPA) Theater Project intern, and together they worked on performances in the attic of his school. Throughout his life, Baldwin maintained a passion for the theater, and even near death he struggled to complete a play entitled *The Welcome Table*.

The Amen Corner. In 1953, Baldwin finished *The Amen Corner*, which deals with the struggles of Sister Margaret, a church leader, to hold together her family and her storefront church. Sister Margaret cannot fully control her rebel son, David, who is determined to leave the church and begin a new artistic life as a musical performer, following in the footsteps of his father, Luke, a jazz musician. Previously, Sister Margaret had striven to protect David from falling into the subterranean world of jazz. Sister Margaret now faces opposition within the church from Sister Moore, Sister Boxer, and Brother

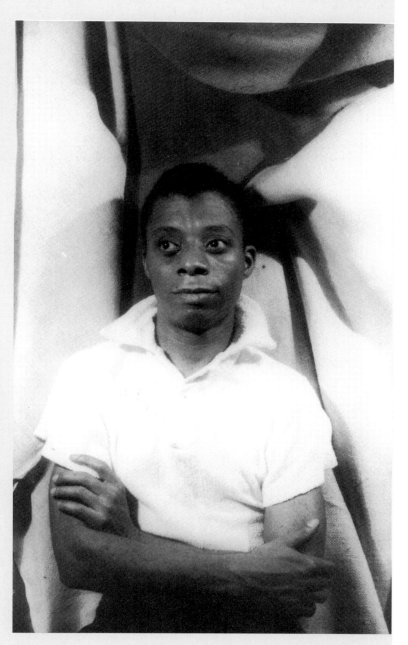

Photographer Carl van Vechten took this photograph of Baldwin around 1950, not long before Baldwin finished writing his play *The Amen Corner*.

A 1954 advertisement for the first production of *The Amen Corner*, which took place at Howard University in Washington, D.C.

Boxer. With the death of Luke and the departure of David, Sister Margaret cannot lead her church, and control falls to her opponents.

The Amen Corner was first performed at Howard University under the direction of Owen Dodson, May 11–14, 1954. This staging was Baldwin's first significant experience in the theater, and reviews in the Washington newspapers were favorable, increasing Baldwin's confidence. The play also advanced the acceptance of the African American dialect because it gave fluent voice to that idiom. On April 16, 1965, *The Amen Corner* opened at the Barrymore Theater in New York, with Beah Richards as Sister Margaret and Frank Silvera as Luke. The play ran for forty-eight performances. Subsequently, there were performances in Europe in 1965 under the joint leadership of Ellis Haizlip and Rudolph Stoiber, with Lloyd Richards directing. In September 1983, at Ford's Theater in Washington,

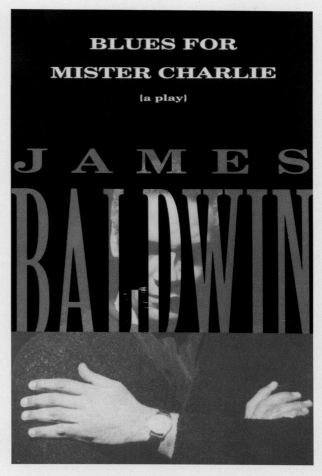

A 1995 cover of Baldwin's play *Blues for Mister Charlie*, published by Vintage Books, a division of Random House.

D.C., Phil Rose directed a six-week run of *The Amen Corner*, which featured Rhetta Hughes as Sister Margaret. In the fall of 1986 in London, another production of *The Amen Corner* ran for several months to sold-out audiences. The cast, which included British and West Indian actors, was directed by Anton Phillips. This success prompted Baldwin to rededicate himself to the writing of *The Welcome Table*.

Blues for Mister Charlie. On April 23, 1964, at the ANTA Theater in New York, Baldwin's play *Blues for Mister Charlie* began its controversial life on the stage. The play was based partly on the murder of Emmett Till, a black youth killed in Mississippi for allegedly whistling at a white woman. In a subsequent trial, Till's murderers were acquitted. The play also made reference to Medgar Evers, the civil rights leader slain in front of his own home on June 12, 1963.

The play begins with the murder of Richard, the son of Meridian Henry, a black minister in Mississippi. Lyle Britten, a white store owner, is unmistakably identified as the murderer, and he himself reveals that his motive is racial hatred. The victim's family struggles to bring the case to trial, and when it does come to court, the murderer is declared innocent. The play raises questions about the differences between God's law and civil law, between genuine justice and the "justice" rendered in the South. The play also examines the division between whites and blacks and the terrifying duality of Lyle, who on one hand is a loving husband and father and on the other hand is a vicious, racist murderer. Finally, the play demonstrates that the struggle for civil rights may be fought nonviolently, but the option of violence cannot be ruled out completely.

The production of *Blues for Mister Charlie* faced several problems. Baldwin and his advisers disagreed about vulgar language, casting, venue, acting approach, and the choice of director. The chosen cast included Rip Torn as Lyle; Diana Sands as Juanita; Al Freeman, Jr., as Richard; Pat Hingle as Parnell; and Percy Rodriguez as Meridian. Burgess Meredith directed. Controversial for its time, the play drew mixed reviews, with some critics finding the attacks on whites difficult to accept. Because Baldwin insisted on keeping ticket prices low, the show's revenues did not cover costs, despite good ticket sales. Special gifts from the Rockefeller family kept the production alive.

In April 1965, a performance of *Blues for Mister Charlie* was staged in London, but it did not feature the original cast, lacked the lighting of the original performance, and drew fiercely negative reviews. In Stockholm in 1965, Ingmar Bergman directed a performance of *Blues for Mister Charlie* with an all-white cast. This performance drew praise from Baldwin, who remarked that "the play is about tribes, not races, how we treat one another."

The Plays as a Key to Baldwin's Work. Despite the tensions that marked Baldwin's contact with the theater, his plays are significant examinations of the human condition and important works in his literary career. Baldwin's life begins and ends in drama, and readers who become familiar with Baldwin's work as a playwright gain a special insight into the dramatic proportions of his novels, stories, and essays.

SOURCES FOR FURTHER STUDY

Baldwin, James. "Notes for Blues." In *Blues for Mister Charlie*. New York: Laurel, 1964.

———. "Notes for *The Amen Corner*." In *The Amen Corner*. New York: Laurel, 1968.

Leeming, David. *James Baldwin: A Biography*. New York: Henry Holt, 1995.

Weatherby, W. J. *James Baldwin: Artist on Fire*. New York: Laurel, 1990.

Werner, Craig, Thomas J. Taylor, and Robert McClenaghan. "James Baldwin." In *Critical Survey of Drama*, edited by Frank N. Magill. Rev. ed. Vol. 1. Pasadena, Calif.: Salem Press, 1994.

Reader's Guide to Major Works

GO TELL IT ON THE MOUNTAIN
Genre: Novel
Subgenre: Family history
Published: New York, 1953
Time period: 1930s
Setting: Harlem, New York; south United States

Themes and Issues. *Go Tell It on the Mountain* is a story of suffering. Deborah is the victim of a rape, and following the rape she is rejected in courtship. Eventually, she marries Gabriel, but he proves unfaithful. She is sickly and dies. Similarly, Elizabeth also suffers: Her tender love with Richard is destroyed by racist law enforcement when he is imprisoned on a fabricated charge and experiences a suicidal depression. Elizabeth gives birth to Richard's child, but after his suicide she must raise the child without a father. Florence loses her hus-

William H. Johnson's oil painting *I Baptize Thee* (The Smithsonian American Art Museum, Washington, D.C.) reflects the religious awakening and spiritual enlightenment of John Grimes, a central character in Baldwin's largely autobiographical novel *Go Tell It on the Mountain*.

band during the war and now faces her own death. Rachel was born a slave and endured numerous abuses before securing her freedom.

Salvation, as well as suffering, is a theme of this novel. While the various characters reveal their sufferings through their prayers, they also reveal their differing capacities for true salvation. Baldwin writes with a perceptive awareness of the possibilities for regeneration and redemption through patience, kindness, and love.

The novel also examines the question of legitimacy and the struggle to establish an identity. John is born out of wedlock, yet is a faithful son and dedicated Christian. Roy, the "legitimate" son, is given to rebellion and sin. Gabriel, despite the plain evidence before him, prefers Roy because he is his biological son.

Go Tell It on the Mountain also affirms righteousness. Elizabeth is kind and self-sacrificing. Florence insists that Gabriel admit the truth about himself and face his family accordingly. Elisha shows support and love for John in his struggle for salvation.

The Plot. *Go Tell It on the Mountain* is a richly autobiographical novel set in a Pentecostal church in Harlem, similar to the one in which Baldwin's stepfather preached. It is centered on a day in the life of fourteen-year-old John Grimes while he is on the "threshing floor" of religious transformation. It also relates the thoughts of John's mother, stepfather, and aunt as each prays in the church. Gabriel Grimes, John's stepfather, as the head of the family and the minister of the church, pits himself forcefully against John.

Years earlier, when Gabriel married John's mother Elizabeth, he accepted her illegitimate child, John, as his own. In spite of his pledge, Gabriel now favors Roy, his "legitimate" son, and scorns John, whom he regards as the product of sin. However, Gabriel hides the fact that years ago in the South, he indulged in adultery, fathered an illegitimate child, and abandoned both mother and child, who subsequently died. In arrogant hypocrisy, Gabriel now condemns Elizabeth and John but conceals his own shame. For him, John is an unbearable reminder of his own infidelity.

Florence, Gabriel's sister, has a letter from Deborah, Gabriel's first wife, which reveals the details of Gabriel's sin. Florence has kept the letter for thirty years, but she has not mentioned it to anyone.

Near the end of the novel Florence confronts Gabriel with the letter, threatening to expose his past and demanding that he treat his wife and stepson fairly. Gabriel, however, feels he has made his peace with the Lord and that he does not need to disclose the truth to John and Elizabeth. John's salvation and triumph override the confrontation between Florence and Gabriel, leaving the reader to speculate about Gabriel's future relationship with his family. Regardless of Gabriel's attitudes toward him, John Grimes achieves spiritual enlightenment, and the novel ends with the promise of his awakened soul.

Analysis. Baldwin achieves strong unity by focusing on one day in the life of one person spent almost entirely in one place. He adds variety with the narratives embodied in the prayers of Florence, Gabriel, and Elizabeth and other churchgoers. These prayer-narratives interrupt the progress toward John's "going through," creating suspense and prolonging the satisfaction the reader takes in John's awakening. Gabriel Grimes is a richly developed character whose sin, hypocrisy, and hatred contrasts with John Grimes's youthful innocence and goodness. Ultimately, John comes to accept and admire Gabriel, despite his hostility toward him. This acceptance is indicative of John's true and authentic spiritual awakening.

SOURCES FOR FURTHER STUDY

"Go Tell It on the Mountain." In *Masterplots II: African American Fiction Series*, edited by Frank N. Magill. Vol. 1. Pasadena, Calif.: Salem Press, 1994.

Harris, Trudier. *Black Women in the Fiction of James Baldwin*. Knoxville: University of Tennessee Press, 1985.

———, ed. *Essays on "Go Tell It on the Mountain."* New York: Cambridge University Press, 1996.

Kinnamon, Keneth, ed. *James Baldwin: A Collection of Critical Essays*. Englewood Cliffs, N.J.: Prentice-Hall, 1974.

"SONNY'S BLUES"

Genre: Short story
Subgenre: Moral tale
Published: 1957
Time period: 1950s
Setting: New York City

Themes and Issues. Although "Sonny's Blues" is set in New York City in the 1950s, it contains timeless moral messages. The narrator has a duty to his younger brother, Sonny, a musician, but he is bitterly disappointed to learn of Sonny's arrest on drug charges. Keeping a promise to his mother to stand by Sonny in his hour of difficulty, the narrator reaches out to him, but their communication is strained and incomplete. Eventually the narrator learns that his own practical approach to life is not the only way to live. Sonny's fulfillment in musical artistry is not as safe and secure as the narrator's own choice to become an algebra teacher, but Sonny must answer a calling. The reconciliation of the brothers occurs when the narrator appreciates Sonny's goal.

The moral dimensions of "Sonny's Blues" are also clear in Sonny's correspondence to the Suffering Servant in the Bible's Book of Isaiah. Sonny's name could be merely a generic nickname, but some readers are inclined to see Sonny as a manifestation of the Son himself, just as readers of the Bible see the Suffering Servant as Jesus. In enduring his brother's slow transformation toward understanding and harmony, Sonny is like the Suffering Servant, who "is despised and rejected of men" yet bears their sorrows and trials and provides healing.

Baldwin's background as a preacher again came in handy when writing his short story "Sonny's Blues." The title of this painting by Romare Bearden, *Tenor Sermon*, echoes both the musical and religious references that are woven into Baldwin's story about a man's gradual acceptance of his brother's calling to be a jazz musician.

The Plot. The unnamed narrator, a high-school algebra teacher, is married and has a daughter. He has little patience for his students, the people in the street, and his own brother, who do not possess his discipline and level of responsibility. The story shows the narrator's step-by-step transformation and spiritual thaw. The first step is the loss of the narrator's child, Grace. From jail, Sonny writes and expresses sympathy, initiating the communication between the two. The second step is conversations between Sonny and the narrator. At first, the narrator is tense and cannot fathom Sonny's aims, and the brotherly connection is almost lost. However, brotherly love prevails, and the narrator begins to understand Sonny's suffering and need for artistic musical expression. Finally, at a jazz performance, the narrator hears his brother's music and recognizes that Sonny's choice is right for him. The brothers are reconciled.

Analysis. "Sonny's Blues" takes its strength from its references to music and the Bible. Music is part of the narrator's family tradition because the narrator's uncle played guitar and sang songs. The brothers carry on the family's interest in jazz music, with the narrator preferring Louis Armstrong and Sonny preferring Charlie Parker. The revival singers in the street add spiritual selections, and their struggle to uplift others with music is parallel to the final effort of Sonny in his performance of "Am I Blue?" at the jazz club.

Baldwin's experience as a preacher and his thorough knowledge of the Bible enable him to incorporate numerous biblical references. God visits Cain to ask where Abel is, and in the same way the narrator's conscience prods the narrator to know where Sonny is. The biblical parable of the Prodigal Son is also called to mind because the narrator is uncomfortable with his father's special love for Sonny in spite of Sonny's wayward behavior. The concluding line of the story refers to "the very cup of trembling," recalling the same phrase in the Book of Isaiah. The source of misunderstanding between the brothers is initially like a cup of trembling, but at the jazz performance, setting the cup aside, Sonny shows that the misunderstanding between the brothers is at an end.

SOURCES FOR FURTHER STUDY

Bieganowski, Ronald. "James Baldwin's Visions of Otherness in 'Sonny's Blues' and *Giovanni's Room.*" *CLA Journal* 32 (September 1988): 69–80.

Mosher, Marlene. "Baldwin's 'Sonny's Blues.'" *Explicator* 40, no. 4 (Summer 1982): 59.

Washington, Mary Helen. "Commentary on James Baldwin: 'Sonny's Blues.'" In *Memory of Kin: Stories About Family by Black Writers*, edited by Mary Helen Washington. New York: Anchor Books, 1991.

"STRANGER IN THE VILLAGE"

Genre: Essay
Subgenre: Social criticism
Published: New York, 1953
Time period: Mid-twentieth century
Setting: Small village in Switzerland

Themes and Issues. This essay recounts James Baldwin's experience as the only black person living in an all-white Swiss village. Although within reach of important cities, the village remains isolated. The residents have never before seen a black man, and they regard Baldwin not as an individual, but as a "Negro." The village children, even in their innocence and enthusiasm, shout "Neger! Neger!" when they see him. They marvel that the color of his skin does not rub off when they touch him and that no electrical shock occurs when they touch his woolly hair. Baldwin understands that the villagers show "no element of intentional unkindness," but is disturbed that they also show no recognition of his status as a fellow human being. To them, he is "simply a human wonder."

Among the adults, one woman proudly reports on their collections of money to aid needy people in Africa, expecting Baldwin to be thankful. Someone suggests that Baldwin might let his hair grow long and use it to fashion a winter coat. Some women turn away from Baldwin when they pass him in the street; others seem to suspect that he is a firewood

This 1957 photograph of student Jefferson Thomas being harassed by a group of white students in Little Rock, Arkansas, reflects the isolation that Baldwin felt when living in an all-white village in Switzerland, a period he discusses in "Stranger in the Village," his 1953 essay about the black person's struggle to be seen as an individual.

thief. Still others teach their children that the devil is black and thereby make them regard Baldwin with terror.

The Essay. Baldwin's focus in "Stranger in the Village" soon shifts to a much broader analysis of black-white relations and the course of history. Baldwin argues that the village, if it were even more remote and primitive, nevertheless would maintain its link to Western civilization. About the villagers he remarks, "The most illiterate among them is related, in a way that I am not, to Dante, Shakespeare, Michelangelo, Aeschylus, Da Vinci, Rembrandt, and Racine; the cathedral at Chartres says something to

them which it cannot say to me, as indeed would New York's Empire State Building." In contrast, the black American lives in a disturbing reality: "He is unique among the black men of the world in that his past was taken from him, almost literally, at one blow." Any effort to trace a black person's family heritage hits a cut-off point when slave records are reached. Thus, Baldwin argues, American blacks must find identity in an American culture or have no identity at all.

The battle for identity is already won, however, because the African American is an American citizen. White society in the United States cannot deny this citizenship; to look on blacks as "strangers in the village" is now impossible. Baldwin ends his troubling essay with a powerful affirmation: "This world is white no longer, and it will never be white again."

Analysis. The argument in "Stranger in the Village" is that the United States, because of its troubled history of racial relations, is unlike any other country. The issues of slavery and race affect the United States in a pervasive and lingering manner. Nevertheless, these obstacles inevitably are overcome. In this essay, the Swiss village is a model for an American society that once existed—one that many Americans, in their struggle to live at peace with their own minds, would like to reestablish. The members of this society, like the members of the Swiss village, make the human individuality of blacks invisible and congratulate themselves for what they think is appropriately noble behavior. Baldwin, as a black man in the village, represents all blacks in America engaged in the struggle to establish their identities and be recognized for their individuality. By assertion, Baldwin concludes that society in the United States is already beyond the point where blacks are invisible and that no reactionary outlooks on racial identity are possible.

Baldwin's eloquence forcefully underscores his ideas. He is impressively literate and stylistically fluent, and his sharpness and wit make any effort to impose invisibility upon him absurd. Baldwin is an American, and American citizens must acknowledge him.

SOURCES FOR FURTHER STUDY

Leeming, David Adams. *James Baldwin: A Biography.* New York: Holt, 1994.

Morrison, Toni, ed. *James Baldwin: Collected Essays.* New York: Library of America, 1998.

Other Works

ANOTHER COUNTRY (1962). This novel places more emphasis on dramatic interaction among characters than on a clearly structured plot. Cass and Richard, Ida and Vivaldo, Eric and Yves, and many other characters meet, drink, smoke, and talk. James Baldwin explores the psychology of attraction and the formation of relationships, and how one establishes one's identity through connection with others. He examines love and laments that few seem ready to pay the dues that love demands. Baldwin asks how various issues such as race, violence, jealousy, the pursuit of art (whether music, writing, or dancing), sexual preference, and infidelity affect a relationship. Baldwin interprets the psychology of human decline and degeneration in the context of sexual connection, ultimately suggesting that true meaning and connection in relationship is possible only when people are willing to be exposed and vulnerable.

THE FIRE NEXT TIME (1963). This book is a two-part essay examining the racial nightmare of the United States. The first part, "My Dungeon Shook: Letter to My Nephew on the One Hundredth Anniversary of the Emancipation," is like a play in which Baldwin publicly addresses his nephew, making his readers his audience. The lesson Baldwin gives to his nephew (and indirectly to his readers) is that society forces lowered expectations on blacks simply because they are black. However, blacks must also learn that individuals, such as the forebears of the Baldwins and other families, can rise above oppression to achieve great things. The painful irony is that Baldwin's letter is written one hundred years after the emancipation of the slaves, and still the racial struggle persists.

In the second part, "Down at the Cross: Letter from a Region in My Mind," Baldwin directly addresses his readers to examine the

Like many of Baldwin's works, particularly his two-part essay *The Fire Next Time*, Michael Escoffery's 1995 painting *400 Years of Our People* reflects the passage of time and the struggles of blacks throughout history.

racial nightmare and suggest a possible solution. Baldwin recalls with fiery indignation the day a bartender refused to serve him a drink because the bartender took Baldwin, then thirty-seven years old, to be underage. Baldwin also recalls the satisfaction he felt in Harlem when the police, who so often relished the opportunity to arouse fear in blacks, found themselves fearful of Black Muslims preaching in the streets.

However, Baldwin, in describing his encounter with Elijah Muhammad, the head of the Black Muslim movement, is skeptical about the practicality of the proposal for the surrender of territory by the United States for the establishment of a separate black nation. Instead, Baldwin calls for "the relatively conscious whites and relatively conscious blacks" to

move the nation forward "to end the racial nightmare." If this purposeful union cannot be forged, then the next ending of the world will not be by water, but by fire.

IF BEALE STREET COULD TALK (1974). This novel describes the love between Fonny and Tish and how each of their families responds to their relationship. The novel also explores the social challenges posed by corrupt law enforcement and an inadequate justice system, demonstrating that those who stand by a falsely accused man must resort to extraordinary measures to keep justice on course. In a seemingly senseless world, love is the force capable of overcoming senselessness. At the same time, the price of love may be the sacrifice of one's morality—as in Tish's readiness to prostitute herself to raise cash for the defense—or of life itself, as in Frank's despondent suicide.

"NOTES OF A NATIVE SON" (1955). The title piece in a collection of essays, this essay describes Baldwin's connection to his stepfather, exploring the tensions between them. Baldwin reveals his desperation to break from the family and church, his maddening frustration in facing racism in the United States, and his sobering acceptance of his stepfather, if only after his death. The breaking of glass is a key conceit throughout the essay: Baldwin angrily throws a glass into a mirror in a restaurant that refuses him service because he is black; he also tells of the broken glass in Harlem streets after a race riot and describes the drive through broken glass to the cemetery for his stepfather's burial.

"PREVIOUS CONDITION" (1948). The narrator of this short story, Peter, finds himself caught between two worlds and cannot fit in either. He cannot live in the white world, where racism makes his individuality imperceptible to whites. In such a world, renting an apartment, having dinner in a restaurant, finding employment, and facing police officers are agonizing and dangerous challenges. Personal relationships are also plagued with difficulties. Peter's relationships with Ida and Jules are especially problematic because they cross both racial and religious boundaries. Ironically, relationships within the black community are sometimes no easier. Near the end of the story, when Peter enters a bar frequented by blacks, he feels no connection to the customers. Despite Peter's alienation in this context, he observes, "A white outsider coming in would have seen a young Negro drinking in a Negro bar, perfectly in his element, in his place, as the saying goes. However, the people here knew differently, as I did. I didn't seem to have a place."

Resources

Information on James Baldwin may be found on audio and video, as well as the World Wide Web. Resources include the following:

Audio Tapes. In an audiotape available from Spoken Arts of New Rochelle, New York, *The View from Here: A National Press Club Address* (1988), James Baldwin addresses the National Press Club. Another audiotape, available from the American Audio Prose Library of Columbia, Missouri, entitled *James Baldwin: Interview with Kay Bonetti* (1984), clarifies views expressed in Baldwin's essays. In an *Interview with James Baldwin* (1979), an audiotape available from Tapes for Readers of Washington, D.C., Baldwin discusses Harlem, the place of his birth, and also refers to his trips to Europe and Africa.

James Baldwin: The Price of the Ticket. This eighty-seven-minute video was directed by Karen Thorsen in 1989 and is available from California Newsreel of San Francisco, California. It is an informative study of the life, works, and career of James Baldwin. Extensive footage of Baldwin reveals him at all stages of his career, and interviews with his family, friends, and literary associates describe the complexity of Baldwin's growth as an artist and activist.

James Baldwin Teacher Resource File. This Web site provides links to biography, bibliography, criticism, and lesson plans. (http://falcon.jmu.edu/~ramseyil/baldwin.htm)

Malaspina Great Books, James Baldwin (1924–1987). This Internet research project by Russell McNeil, is an interactive database of great figures in literature and the arts. The research page on James Baldwin features a bibliography and numerous links to other sites. (http://www.mala.bc.ca/~mcneil/baldwin.htm)

WILLIAM T. LAWLOR

Saul Bellow

BORN: June 10, 1915, Lachine, Canada
IDENTIFICATION: Late twentieth-century novelist known for his stories of intellectual characters who have trouble coping with life's obstacles.

Saul Bellow's work spans five decades and many different types of fiction. One of his most popular works, *Seize the Day* (1956), concerns a failed salesman living on the Upper West Side of Manhattan who loses all his money yet manages to gain a sense of feeling and connection with the world. Bellow has also written long, highly ambitious works that tie together mundane personal struggles with major themes in American civilization and the history of the modern world. He writes about both individuals and their social backgrounds. The importance of his work was recognized when he was awarded the Nobel Prize in Literature in 1976. Bellow's novels are considered central to the course of modern American fiction.

The Writer's Life

Solomon (Saul) Bellow was born on June 10, 1915, in Lachine, Quebec, a suburb of Montreal. His parents were Russian Jewish immigrants, and he grew up with his three siblings in an almost exclusively Jewish neighborhood.

Bellow began to think of himself as a writer at the age of eight, when he was hospitalized for peritonitis and pneumonia and came close to death. These illnesses had their compensation in his exposure to the hospital reading room. He read books such as Anna Sewell's *Black Beauty* (1877) and, particularly, the New Testament. As a Jew, Bellow did not believe in the New Testament in a religious sense, and he hid from his parents the fact that he read it. Nevertheless, his fascination with Jesus Christ was one of the spurs that led him to identify writing as his future career.

Man of Chicago. In 1924 Bellow moved with his family to Chicago. Although he was not born there, he became one of its most famous voices, and Chicago is very much his city. He graduated from Tuley High School and did his undergraduate work at Northwestern University, just outside Chicago. His major was in anthropology, a comparatively young discipline that provided background for his insight into the way people live and his interest in cultural contexts. He took classes from, among others, the noted anthropologist Melville J. Herskovits.

Bellow married upon graduation from college. After a brief stint of graduate work at the University of Wisconsin, he decided that he did not want to be an academic and decided upon writing as a career. After moving to New York, he published his first novel, *Dangling Man*, in 1944. Though it met with mixed reviews, it was immediately clear that Bellow was a writer who commanded attention.

In the late 1940s and the 1950s Bellow taught at various universities in the Northeast and Midwest, and he made friends with many figures in the literary establishment, particularly that group centered around the magazine *Partisan Review*. *Partisan Review* was a famous magazine that combined an appreciation of modern trends in literature with a left-wing political posi-

Nicola Victor Ziroli's 1934 painting *Bridges in Winter* depicts a snowy crossing in Bellow's beloved city, Chicago, Illinois. Although Bellow was born in Canada, his writing often highlights Chicago, leading many to think of Bellow as Chicago's native son.

tion. Bellow had many friends in this group and was often seen as a member. However, Bellow always maintained his independence from this group and is notable as much for his differences from the *Partisan Review* consensus as his participation in it. Some of this difference came from the fact that Bellow never saw himself as a "New York intellectual." His roots were in Chicago, both in a geographical and spiritual sense. Like many people of Chicago, Bellow had a good work ethic, which helped his productivity as a writer. While his New York colleagues argued and debated, Bellow kept producing lengthy, ambitious novels.

Leading American Novelist.

During the 1950s Bellow began to attain fame as a novelist. He won the National Book Award in 1954 for *The Adventures of Augie March* (1953). He tried to make a cultural impact outside novel-writing by coediting a literary journal, *The Noble Savage*. Though this magazine was well regarded, it did not prosper financially and ceased publication in 1963. Thereafter Bellow continued with his own writing.

Sweden's King Carl Gustaf (right) presents the Nobel Prize for Literature to Bellow in Stockholm on December 10, 1976.

His 1964 best-seller, *Herzog*, made him a household name among American readers. During this period, though, Bellow's life was troubled, with several divorces following marriages that produced three sons by different mothers.

In 1962 Bellow reestablished his identity with Chicago by accepting a position on the renowned Committee on Social Thought at the University of Chicago. This did not confine him to teaching only literature, but let him explore a range of interests across cultural disci-

plines. Even as he attained great heights of popularity and fame, Bellow offended more liberal critics and readers with his critical attitude toward the youth movement and political radicalism of the 1960s. He was thought to be behind the times, not in touch with new currents in American culture.

Nobel Prize.

While some may have doubted Bellow's timeliness, few ever doubted his stature, which was confirmed by the strongly positive reception given his novel *Humboldt's*

HIGHLIGHTS IN BELLOW'S LIFE

1915   Saul Bellow is born Solomon Bellows on June 10 in Lachine, Quebec.

1924   Family moves to Chicago.

1933   Bellow graduates from Tuley High School.

1937   Marries Anita Goshkin (later divorced); receives bachelor's degree from Northwestern University.

1943   Son Gregory is born.

1944   Bellow publishes first novel, *Dangling Man.*

1945   Serves in the United States Merchant Marine.

1954   Wins National Book Award for *The Adventures of Augie March.*

1956   Marries Alexandra Tschacbasov (later divorced).

1957   Son Adam is born.

1960–1963 Bellow coedits journal *The Noble Savage.*

1961   Marries Susan Glassman (later divorced).

1962   Joins Committee on Social Thought, University of Chicago.

1964   Son Daniel is born.

1968   Bellow is decorated with France's Croix de Chevalier.

1974   Marries Alexandra Ionesco Tulcea (later divorced).

1976   Bellow is awarded Pulitzer Prize for fiction and Nobel Prize in Literature.

1980   Receives O. Henry Award for short story "A Silver Dish."

1988   Receives Italy's Presto Scanno Award.

1989   Marries Janis Freedman.

1990   Bellow is Romines Lecturer at Oxford University in England.

1993   Accepts professorship at Boston University.

1995   Cofounds journal *News from the Republic of Letters.*

1998   Wins Jewish Medal for the Arts.

SAUL BELLOW

*The Adventures of
Augie March*

Bellow places his eyeglasses back in their case after giving a reading at the Goodman Theater in Chicago, Illinois, on October 25, 1982.

Bellow encountered an old friend from high school and, after a long discussion reminiscing about old mutual acquaintances, the friend asked Bellow, in all innocence, how he was making a living.

A New Phase of Life.

Bellow's next novel, *The Dean's December* (1982), was poorly received by critics. They saw it as too political and too much a vehicle for Bellow's own opinions. The book was noteworthy for its affirmative portrayal of a female character, a Romanian scientist thought to be closely based on Bellow's fourth wife, Alexandra Ionesco Tulcea, whom he had married in 1974. Any sense of romantic bliss was premature, though, as the couple separated in 1986 and divorced shortly thereafter. Through these changes, Bellow continued to write, but his novels were less large-scale.

In 1993 Bellow surprised many people by leaving Chicago to assume a post as professor of literature at Boston University.

Gift (1975). It not only won a Pulitzer Prize for best novel by an American but contributed to Bellow's receiving the Nobel Prize for the entire body of his work. In December of 1976 Bellow traveled to Sweden with several family members to receive the award. He gave a well-received speech concerning the influences upon him as a novelist and a person.

Bellow's success did not go to his head. He told two stories concerning this: For twenty years, he had said "hello" every morning to a policeman on the street near his Chicago residence. The day after he received the prize, he walked past the policeman, and they greeted each other as if nothing had changed. Similarly,

This move, combined with his marriage in 1989 to Janis Freedman, seemed to herald a new phase in Bellow's life. Bellow's duties at Boston University included giving public lectures and teaching a freshman seminar on nineteenth-century European fiction. The university also supported Bellow's launch of a new literary journal, *News from the Republic of Letters*, coedited with longtime friend Keith Botsford. Bellow also devoted time to his own fiction and nonfiction. Even in his mid-eighties, Bellow continued to lead a life truly dedicated to the work of literature—reading, teaching, and above all writing.

The Writer's Work

An intellectual writer, a Jewish writer, and a modern writer, Saul Bellow is each and all of these things in his own way. People coming to his novels expecting ingrained stereotypes are likely to walk away baffled. Throughout a long and distinguished career, Bellow developed a style and an outlook peculiarly his own.

The Head and the Heart. Bellow transcends time, place, and ethnicity to write about humanity in all its glory and pain. Though his heroes are often learned, successful men, they equally often have not solved the most basic problems of life, such as love, values, and identity. To Bellow's heroes, the problems of the mind may seem complex, yet they are solvable—with a certain level of background, training, and intellectual temperament. The problems of the heart, on the other hand, however simple in outline, seem impossible for them to solve. Bellow's heroes are constantly challenged by moral crises.

Bellow puts so many learned references in his work that reading his novels can be an education in itself. Readers are especially likely to learn about modern European society and philosophy, although Bellow is interested in much else besides. However, a purely intellectual approach to Saul Bellow's work is probably mistaken. Bellow's characters are people with as

Many of Bellow's characters are highly intelligent and successful men who lack a true sense of identity. On an emotional level, they try to blend in with their surroundings in an effort to protect themselves, as reflected in this twentieth-century painting by Ben Shahn.

SOME INSPIRATIONS BEHIND BELLOW'S WORK

Much of Saul Bellow's fiction is set in Chicago, and this gritty, blue-collar city has had a great impact on his work. Growing up in Chicago exposed Bellow to many different types of people, from university professors to local hoodlums and working-class men and women of many ethnicities. Chicago gave Bellow a sense of a varied social tableau. Whereas many writers know only "their own sort" of people, Bellow's wide social experience allows him to take any aspect of life as his potential subject. He can describe a group of subway commuters waiting for a train with as much depth as he can describe a group of intellectuals arguing about literature. Even when Bellow writes about the more outwardly glamorous city of New York, as in *Seize the Day*, he focuses on ordinary people such as Tommy Wilhelm.

Bellow's undergraduate and graduate academic work was not in literature, but in anthropology. The study of "humankind," anthropology focuses on everyday life and comparative social structures, not great historical events. Bellow's anthropology training plays a role in *Henderson the Rain King*, where he is looking at a fictional version of a foreign continent, Africa. His works about ordinary American life also employ a detached yet appreciative anthropological perspective. His study of other people is empathetic as well as systematic; he observes what they do and understands the cultural patterns prompting their behavior.

Some of Bellow's personal friends and acquaintances provided inspiration for his work. For example, his friend the poet Delmore Schwartz is widely agreed to be the character model for Von Humboldt Fleisher in *Humboldt's Gift*. Despite considerable differences between the two men, they had a deep friendship. Like Humboldt, Schwartz was a talented poet who became famous early in his life and foundered in middle age, succumbing to the pressures exerted by American life upon talented artists. Bellow, in contrast, is above all a survivor, willing to negotiate with society, swimming both with and against the cultural tide as needed. These differences of character and fate do not prevent Bellow from giving a finely tuned, sympathetic portrait of Schwartz.

Another friend of Bellow's was Allan Bloom, a professor of political science at the University of Chicago. Bloom produced a national best-seller, *The Closing of the American Mind* (1987), to which Bellow contributed a prologue. Bloom took his philosophical knowledge and ideology in a more straightforward and serious way than Bellow. Despite their very different personalities, the two men were close friends. Bloom was younger than Bellow, but like Delmore Schwartz, he predeceased the novelist. Bellow commented on their friendship in a thinly fictionalized memoir, which he provisionally entitled *Ravelstein* in 2000.

Svenska Akademien
har vid sitt sammanträde
den 21 oktober 1976
i överensstämmelse med
föreskrifterna i det av
ALFRED NOBEL
den 27 november 1895
upprättade testamente
beslutat att tilldela

Saul Bellow

1976 års nobelpris i litteratur
för den mänskliga förståelse
och subtila kulturanalys
som förenas i hans verk.

STOCKHOLM DEN 10 DECEMBER 1976

The actual Nobel Prize painting and award that were presented to Bellow in Sweden. *Humboldt's Gift*, Bellow's Pulitzer Prize–winning novel about the friendship of two writers, contributed to Bellow's receiving the Nobel Prize for the body of his work. The word *Humboldt* can be seen on the right half of the painting.

much need for love and emotional sustenance as anyone else. Their intellectual accomplishments do not make them immune from tragedy, loss, and heartbreak. To explore Bellow's imaginative universe requires both the mind and the heart.

Jewish Themes. Bellow's generation of Jewish writers in the United States was the first to receive widespread media exposure and cultural coverage. Bellow wrote his major work in an era when Jews were rapidly being accepted into the mainstream of American society. His main characters are usually Jews, with the prominent exception of the title character in *Henderson the Rain King* (1959). Bellow has re-

fused, however, to make his Jewish identity the center of his literary profile. He has said that he prefers to be seen as an American, rather than a Jewish, writer.

Though rarely involved in Jewish religious practice, Bellow's Jewish background has contributed to the profound understanding of human victimization and the idea of the victim in his novels. His Jewish identity is also reflected in his nonfiction book on his visit to Israel, *To Jerusalem and Back: A Personal Account* (1976), and in his reporting on the Arab-Israeli wars and the Camp David peace treaty for the New York-area newspaper *Newsday*. The suffering experienced by Jews through the ages, and particularly in the twentieth century, gives added force to a sense of shared humanity that often is evident in Bellow's fiction. The tradition of Jewish humor also may have influenced Bellow; even when he is being very serious, he is often a considerably funnier writer than he is usually deemed.

Modern Men. Although Bellow's style is sometimes seen as traditional, his heroes are very modern in their needs and preoccupations. They seem not to possess any ingrown identity and often take on the emotional coloration of their surroundings as a sort of protective measure. Their relationships with women often seem driven less by emotional or physical need than by the sense that the women with whom they are involved can confer a sort of identity on them. Other possible sources of identity include allegiance to political causes, participation in criminal activities, and expeditions into remote wildernesses. Bellow is never optimistic that his heroes can find identities outside themselves. Many of his novels suggest that the only true source of identity is the often ungratifying one of sober self-knowledge. However, some of his later works end in more conventional romantic resolutions that might suggest otherwise.

Bellow and Women. Even Bellow's admirers concede that his female characters are less interesting than his male characters. Whereas

Some of Bellow's characters seek to gain identity in their devotion to politics or on their expeditions into the wilderness, and some even resort to criminal activities, as mirrored in Ben Shahn's 1932 painting of Bartolomeo Vanzetti (left) and Nicola Sacco, the Italian immigrants and anarchists found guilty of murder, some feel wrongly, in 1927.

LONG FICTION

1944 Dangling Man
1947 The Victim
1953 The Adventures of Augie March
1956 Seize the Day
1959 Henderson the Rain King
1964 Herzog
1970 Mr. Sammler's Planet
1975 Humboldt's Gift
1982 The Dean's December
1987 More Die of Heartbreak
1989 A Theft
1989 The Bellarosa Connection
1997 The Actual
2000 Ravelstein

SHORT FICTION

1968 Mosby's Memoirs and Other Stories
1984 Him with His Foot in His Mouth and Other Stories
1991 Something to Remember Me By: Three Tales

NONFICTION

1976 To Jerusalem and Back: A Personal Account
1994 It All Ends Up: From the Dim Past to the Uncertain Future

PLAYS

1954 The Wrecker
1964 The Last Analysis
1966 Under the Weather (also known as The Bellow Plays; includes Out from Under, A Wen, and Orange Soufflé)

other male novelists have produced some memorable heroines, Bellow's women tend to be foils or complements for the men who dominate the action. Some commentators have claimed that Bellow's men misuse or exploit women. Many reviewers have even termed Bellow misogynistic, that is, antagonistic toward women. Though some female characters, such as Ramona the flower girl in *Herzog*, have the potential to be appealing figures, Bellow portrays them so much in terms of what they can give to the men in their lives as to be denied any independent basis for existence.

Other female characters, such as the ex-wife in *Humboldt's Gift*, are seen in wholly negative terms. Bellow's defenders might point to more romantic and affirmative portraits in some of Bellow's

SAUL BELLOW

Henderson the Rain King

later, shorter work, such as the character of Amy Wustrin in *The Actual* (1997). However, it should be noted that Bellow's male heroes have trouble with all of humanity, not only with women. Nevertheless, the lack of depth in Bellow's women characters is a definite issue that needs to be dealt with by any serious reader of his fiction.

The Theme of Success and Failure.

Bellow's characters are often self-made men who have risen to prominent positions within American society. They have vast amounts of energy and drive and are for the most part well known and well regarded by their peers. However, they feel unsuccessful or dissatisfied with the success they do have. They also are bewildered by friends who seem to admire them exclusively for their success, and they suspect that they would be far less popular if they were less successful. For characters such as Moses Herzog in *Herzog* and Charlie Citrine in *Humboldt's Gift*, success is less a mark of distinction than something that makes them marked men, ripe for exploitation by hangers-on and opportunists.

On the other hand, a seeming failure such as Tommy Wilhelm in *Seize the Day* (1956) is depicted positively by Bellow even though his life is a complete wreck. Wilhelm at least has some sort of basis for feeling his own pain, his own humanity. In chronicling the stories of poor city boys who have made good, Bellow narrates a major strand of the American Dream, but he does not lose sight of the fact that all people live in similar moral situations and are measured as much by the way they deal with these situations as by any standards of worldly success.

Bellow's Legacy. Saul Bellow was one of the most famous and well-regarded writers of the

twentieth century. His works are frequently taught in college and high school classes. The prominence of *Seize the Day* in high school curricula testifies to the extent of his work's reception.

Although Bellow is a writer of great depth and insight, his works can be enjoyed even by those who do not understand his many literary and cultural references. His tone is sometimes fierce, sometimes meditative, but always good-natured. General readers seem to like Bellow's writing, although it is more complicated than that of many traditionally popular authors. Indeed, Bellow is one of the preeminent cerebral novelists of twentieth-century American fiction; few writers' characters spend as much of their time thinking as his.

BIBLIOGRAPHY

Bach, Gerhard, and Gloria Cronin. *Small Planets: Saul Bellow and the Art of Short Fiction*. East Lansing: Michigan State University Press, 2000.

Braham, Jeanne. *A Sort of Columbus: The American Voyages of Saul Bellow's Fiction*. Athens: University of Georgia Press, 1984.

Harris, Mark. *Saul Bellow: Drumlin Woodchuck*. Athens: University of Georgia Press, 1980.

Hollahan, Eugene, ed. *Saul Bellow and the Struggle at the Center*. New York: AMS Press, 1998.

Hyland, Peter. *Saul Bellow*. New York: St. Martin's Press, 1992.

Kiernan, Robert F. *Saul Bellow*. New York: Continuum, 1989.

Miller, Ruth. *Saul Bellow: Biography of the Imagination*. New York: St. Martin's Press, 1991.

Newman, Judie. *Saul Bellow and History*. New York: St. Martin's Press, 1984.

Opdahl, Keith. *The Novels of Saul Bellow: An Introduction*. University Park: Pennsylvania State University Press, 1968.

Wilson, Jonathan, *On Bellow's Planet: Readings from the Dark Side*, Rutherford, N.J.: Fairleigh Dickinson University Press, 1985.

Reader's Guide to Major Works

HERZOG

Genre: Novel
Subgenre: Psychological realism
Published: New York, 1964
Time period: 1960s
Setting: New York City; Chicago, Illinois; the Berkshires of Massachusetts

Themes and Issues. *Herzog* is one of the great novels of the modern city. Saul Bellow depicts the urban unrest of both New York and Chicago, where people of all classes and vocations seek to find meaning. The story concerns one man's intellectual crisis, but it also addresses more abstract conditions. Moses Herzog, the central character, is a social thinker, and many of his views on the ills of modern society are meant to be taken seriously.

Bellow is adept at embodying in his protagonists and their concrete moral situations the drifting and rootless nature of modern humanity. His character Herzog has so little control of his life, his mind, and his impulses that he seems neither serious nor sympathetic. The novel is not full of action, and much of its drama is waged in the form of ideas, not deeds. Readers used to conventionally exciting plots may find the book dry and boring, but *Herzog* is ultimately Bellow's most psychologically probing novel, penetrating its characters' desires and fears.

The Plot. When Moses Herzog's wife Madeleine leaves him for Valentine Gersbach, his best friend, he finds that he can no longer live his usual life. He begins to write letters to various famous people, to people living and dead, to people he knows, and to people he

Herzog, the main character of Bellow's novel by the same name, uses letter writing as a form of therapy. Although he writes to many, his letters are really intended for no one, as reflected in Will Crocker's image of an envelope without a destination.

The roaming eye of the bride and the uncharacteristic red angel in Marc Chagall's *The Wedding* foreshadow the impending doom of a marriage, which Bellow implies is a contributing factor in the breakdown of modern society in the novel *Herzog*.

does not know. The letters are intended less for their supposed recipients than as vehicles through which Herzog addresses the plight in which he finds himself. Although a brilliant man, Herzog suspects himself of mental instability. He is filled with vengeful emotions toward his wife and her new lover. He goes to Chicago intending to kill both of them, but when he sees Gersbach bathing his own (Herzog's) baby daughter, June, he is touched that Gersbach would show such love and care for a child that is not his own, and he realizes that he cannot harm anyone. Though Herzog still hates Gersbach, he begins to understand how love can bind as well as es-

trange. In this way, he is saved from madness and total disintegration.

At the end of the book, Herzog is happily ensconced in his country home in the Berkshires of Massachusetts. His relationship with his new girlfriend, Ramona the flower girl, seems to be going well. More important, he no longer feels the need to write letters. His mental anguish has been cured.

Analysis. Herzog's tortured attempts to explain to himself the failure of his marriage to Madeleine and his efforts to gain custody of June reflect a central issue in the novel. Bellow is commenting on the increasing prominence of divorce as a social phenomenon, as the once-stable American family structure gives way to tumult and uncertainty. Likewise, Herzog's world, as well as his sanity, is disintegrating around him. Bellow is also sensitive to the plight of young children whose parents are divorced for reasons they do not understand. When Herzog, in a bizarre sequence, is arrested in front of his child, his pain—as well as his daughter's—is wrenchingly conveyed.

Although the novel is full of abstract thoughts on the breakdown of modern society, this theme does not fully resonate until it is embodied in the breakup of one family— Herzog's. *Herzog* portrays the devastation that divorce can cause for both parents and children. The end of a marriage is, for Herzog, not just the end of an emotional relationship but also the shattering of his entire identity. All Herzog's intellectual equipment is barely equal to this level of damage.

Bellow is more than a domestic novelist. He shows how personal crises affect the entire shape of culture, and how widely their impact can resonate, as Herzog's personal troubles genuinely and meaningfully affect his intellectual posture.

SOURCES FOR FURTHER READING

Bigler, Walter. *Figures of Madness in Saul Bellow's Longer Fiction*. New York: Peter Lang, 1998.

Goldman, L. H. *Saul Bellow's Moral Vision*. New York: Irvington, 1983.

Wilson, Jonathan. *Herzog: The Limits of Ideas*. Boston: Twayne Publishers, 1990.

HUMBOLDT'S GIFT

Genre: Novel
Subgenre: Philosophical quest
Published: New York, 1975
Time period: 1930s to 1960s
Setting: New York City; Chicago, Illinois

Themes and Issues. This is Bellow's most ambitious novel. It concerns the friendship between the narrator, Charlie Citrine, a veteran journalist and cultural historian, and his recently deceased friend, the poet Von Humboldt Fleisher.

Charlie had looked up to Humboldt ever since he had made a pilgrimage to the poet's Greenwich Village home as a young man. The relationship between the two writers encompasses many levels of existence, ranging from petty literary jealousies to profound spiritual quests.

One of the themes of the novel is friendship, and how a deep friendship can help one achieve true identity. The replenishing and educative effect of memory is another major emphasis of the book. Humboldt is dead in the literal sense, but, true to the spiritual teachings he has assimilated, Charlie now is able to appreciate his living essence even after his physical death.

The Plot. Humboldt's personal problems and unconventional lifestyle doom him to mental instability, manifested in his increasing jealousy of the more smoothly functioning Charlie. He maliciously cashes a blank check that Charlie gave him to use only in an emergency. Humboldt fills in a large amount, not particularly to steal money from Charlie, but to comment on his belief that, in writing a successful but superficial play that gets good reviews on Broadway, Humboldt has "sold out" to the intellectual establishment. Humboldt then dies in squalor. However, he leaves Charlie a legacy: two screenplays that not only promise to bring Charlie wealth but also serve as a final chapter in the friendship between the two writers.

Charlie is not without his own problems. He is being sued by his ex-wife in a bitter divorce case. He has a new girlfriend, Renata, but is unsure of her affection. His splendid car has been battered by Rinaldo Cantabile, a Mafia operative, over a poker dispute. Charlie's thuggish earthliness is in a sense the opposite of Humboldt's soaring intellect. However, Cantabile's wife is writing a dissertation on Humboldt's work, suggesting that the worlds of the two men are not utterly opposed.

Analysis. Charlie Citrine is very different from Humboldt, but he is able to appreciate his friend's vision and integrity. In a sense,

Humboldt and Charlie are complementary aspects of a unified self. Charlie is practical, sensible, and realistic, whereas Humboldt was intellectual and idealistic. Charlie, in a sense, yearns to be more like Humboldt; he wants to be more spiritual. By the end of the novel, Charlie has been abandoned by Renata and has renounced any rights to the income from Humboldt's film scripts. Despite the many distractions and obstacles that crop up in the course of the narrative, Charlie comes to a far greater understanding of his friend and, even more important, of himself. He is finally able to concentrate upon his own goals. By refusing the proceeds from the film scripts, Charlie integrates Humboldt's idealism into his own practicality.

SOURCES FOR FURTHER READING

Gullette, Margaret Morgenroth. *Safe at Last in the Middle Years.* Berkeley: University of California Press, 1988.

McConnell, Frank. *Four Postwar American Novelists.* Chicago: University of Chicago Press, 1977.

Rodrigues, Eusebio L., *Quest for the Human: An Exploration of Saul Bellow's Fiction.* Lewisburg, Ohio: Bucknell University Press, 1981.

SEIZE THE DAY

Genre: Short novel
Subgenre: Social realism
Published: New York, 1956
Time period: Mid-1950s
Setting: New York City's upper West Side

Themes and Issues. Bellow's most popular work, *Seize the Day* is found frequently on high school and college reading lists. Unlike most of Bellow's novels, it is a tightly knit unit, with a central dilemma that the whole of the story strives to illuminate. It is also a very readable short novel with much substance to debate and discuss. Set in a seedy hotel in the middle of the busiest and most anonymous section of New York, it delineates universal themes of self-worth and compassion. At first Tommy Wilhelm seems pitiful, but then it becomes apparent that he has reached a level of genuine feeling to which few people ever penetrate.

The Plot. Tommy Wilhelm is a forty-four-year-old salesman who is struggling to stay afloat economically and in every other way. He is being swindled by the commodities trader and con man Tamkin. Wilhelm, who has changed his last name in a gesture of self-assertion, is also dominated by his overbearing father, Dr. Adler. Dr. Adler is dis-

Wilhelm's emotional breakthrough, a pivotal turning point in Bellow's novel *Seize the Day*, transforms Wilhelm from a pitiful character to one the reader can admire. Jose Clemente Orozco's drawing *The Sob* reflects Wilhelm's long-awaited, yet surprising, expression of compassion.

appointed in his son and withholds affection from him. Because Dr. Adler and his son both live in the same quasi-rundown hotel in New York City's upper West Side, they are thrown into frequent, uneasy contact with each other.

Wilhelm is handsome enough to have tried once to be a film star. He is intelligent and energetic, but somehow he has never been able to "make anything" of himself in worldly terms. By contrast, Tamkin is a successful con man precisely because he seems to be something more. Using the language of psychology, he acts as if his commodity trading in rye futures is a great artistic project, and that Wilhelm's life will be enriched if he joins in it. Making up for Dr. Adler's coldness, Tamkin is a sort of surrogate father to Wilhelm. Wilhelm knows that Tamkin is going to swindle him but accepts his loss fatalistically. At the end of the book, Wilhelm, wiped out financially, stumbles upon a stranger's funeral. His uncontrolled weeping gives the mourners the impression he is the brother of the deceased, except he does not look at all like him. Utterly anonymous, Wilhelm has an emotional breakthrough. Although Wilhelm, more than ever, seems to be beaten down by life, his compassion for others gives him dignity that arouses the reader's compassion.

Analysis. The title of the book relates to Wilhelm's story in a significant way. "Seize the day" is the English equivalent of the Latin phrase *carpe diem*. This phrase is usually taken to mean something like "Have fun now, for time is passing." Wilhelm does not "seize the day" in this pleasure-seeking sense, but he does learn how to value the lives of the people around him, and thus attains a more profound insight. He is not a hero in the conventional sense, but in facing up to his own desperation he ultimately achieves an integrity for which he can be admired. In contrast, smooth-talking "successes" such as Tamkin are profoundly out of touch with their own humanity.

SOURCES FOR FURTHER READING

Clayton, John. *Saul Bellow: In Defense of Man.* Bloomington: Indiana University Press, 1968.

Kramer, Michael F. *New Essays on "Seize the Day."* New York: Cambridge University Press, 1998.

McCadden, Joseph F. *The Flight from Women in the Fiction of Saul Bellow.* Lanham, Md.: University Press of America, 1980.

Pifer, Ellen. *Saul Bellow Against the Grain.* Philadelphia: University of Pennsylvania Press, 1990.

Other Works

THE ACTUAL (1997). Although this short novel was well received, it was not seen as one of Saul Bellow's major achievements. Its protagonist, Harry Trellman, is an art appraiser who has worked in various trades, both licit and illicit, throughout his long career. He has always been in love with Amy, his high school sweetheart, who has married a man named Jay Wustrin. When Harry, in old age, is employed by the eccentric multimillionaire Adletsky, he comes into contact with Amy once again. After Jay Wustrin dies, Harry confesses his love to Amy at the cemetery where her late husband is being buried.

This tender and sentimental story stands in contrast to the often vitriolic and disgruntled view of women and love featured in many of Bellow's earlier novels. *The Actual* reveals a more graceful and optimistic side of Bellow, demonstrating how an author's body of work can reflect new depth and dimension as age adds wisdom and experience.

THE BELLAROSA CONNECTION (1989). The narrator of this novella is an elderly Jewish man who has made millions through his leadership of the Mnemosyne Institute, a founda-

Hope is expressed in this drawing of trees and butterflies created by a Jewish child in the concentration camp at Terezin in the former Czechoslovakia. Bellow's novel *The Bellarosa Connection*, which focuses on the gratitude of a survivor, is Bellow's tribute to those who survived the Holocaust.

tion that helps people find ways to remember information better. He is a distant relative of a man called Fonstein. Fonstein was a refugee from 1930s Germany who had been rescued from Nazi persecution by the intervention of Billy Rose, a successful theatrical entrepreneur. He came to America, married, and settled into a life of placid contentment.

Fonstein's deep wish was to meet Billy Rose in person and thank him for his generous gesture. Billy Rose, however, cared for the refugees only in the abstract and was not interested in meeting them personally, so he refused Fonstein's constant requests for a meeting. Fonstein's wife was not satisfied with his refusals and tricked Billy Rose into

meeting with her. This meeting, symbolically, took place in Jerusalem, in an Israel that had emerged from the wreck of Jewish suffering in the Holocaust. Fonstein's wife had collected damaging information about Billy Rose with the purpose of blackmailing him into meeting with her husband. After these papers flew out a window accidentally, the meeting never occurred. Nevertheless, this incident brought some degree of closure to the entire situation.

Recalling this story, the narrator tries to get back in touch with the Fonsteins, whom he has not seen for decades. He manages to contact a friend of their son, who informs him that the Fonsteins are both dead. Although neither the narrator nor the son's friend knew the Fonsteins well, their conversation is a kind of belated tribute to the ordinary, yet noteworthy, story of their lives.

Bellow has commented that *The Bellarosa Connection* is his response to the realization that he had not paid sufficient attention to the Holocaust and its devastating effect on twentieth-century culture. This story, written late in his life, is his act of witness to the sufferings of victims of the Holocaust. It is his tribute to the legacy of those who survived the Holocaust, in imaginative as well as literal terms. As in much of Bellow's work, the novel is filled with allusions and complexly worded sentences. However, they do not encumber the story's basic and compelling message.

THE DEAN'S DECEMBER (1982). Along with Mr. Sammler's Planet (1970), The Dean's December is one of Bellow's most explicitly political novels. In both novels, the protagonists bemoan the future of long-established cultural standards in light of the self-indulgent and fraudulent ideologies that they see as characteristic of their times.

The Dean's December features Albert Corde, a dean at the University of Chicago who is married to a Romanian woman (as Bellow himself once was). Corde writes a controversial article for an American magazine, lamenting the decline of Chicago and the tawdry nature of its civil institutions. However, when he visits the then-communist country of Romania to help care for his dying mother-in-law, he finds a society where no complaint of any sort is allowed. He wonders which is worse: the ruthless suppression of all social protest, or the anything-goes ethic of a decaying United States. Corde ultimately chooses the former. Corde's wife's interest in astronomy allows for descriptions of awe-inspiring outer-space vistas, providing at least a momentary counterpoint to the flawed situation of humankind on earth.

HENDERSON THE RAIN KING (1959). This novel's Eugene Henderson seems to be a man who has everything. A successful Connecticut businessman, he could easily be taken as an example of American male confidence at its zenith. It seems surprising, then, that he suddenly gives up everything to embark upon an expedition to Africa.

Henderson is a generous man, but also somewhat naïve. When he encounters the (fictional) Arnewi and Wariri peoples of east central Africa, he makes numerous presuppositions that eventually confound him. He rids the Arnewi of frogs that are contaminating the water supply and ends up destroying their reservoir. He idealizes the Wariri king Dahfu as a kind of representative of the primitive unconscious. However, Dahfu is a scientifically trained doctor who speaks to Henderson in English.

Henderson the Rain King has never been popular among critics. Some critics think that Bellow never should have left his "home territory" of urban-American fiction and set a novel in the alien lands of Africa. Others suggest that the African setting was an interesting innovation, which successfully utilized Bellow's training in anthropology. Although the book is not, and does not try to be, empirically accurate about Africa, Henderson's experience convincingly simulates the process of understanding a culture different from one's own.

MORE DIE OF HEARTBREAK (1987). This is one of Bellow's more intimate novels, lacking the social breadth of works such as *Humboldt's Gift* and focusing on a narrow set of characters and their relationships. Its title refers to the proposition that more people die from heartbreak than from accidents, diseases, and other causes. The characters are uncles and nephews. Benn Crader is a world-famous botanist whose uncle, Harold Vilitzer, is a corrupt backroom politician and whose nephew, Kenneth Trachtenberg, is an academic in his early thirties. Benn falls in love with Matilda Layamon, whom he believes will provide him with a badly needed connection to the world. Matilda, however, turns out to be a limited woman who is only interested in Benn to exploit and take advantage of him.

Moses Soyer's oil-on-canvas painting *Two Men* (Hunter Museum of American Art, Chattanooga, Tennessee) depicts the kinship and isolation felt by uncles and nephews in Bellow's intimate novel *More Die of Heartbreak*.

Kenneth also has problems with women, and he has fathered an illegitimate child by his girlfriend, Treckie.

Bellow, often criticized for using his protagonists simply as voices for his own views, here takes the unusual step of basically splitting his main character into two. Benn and Kenneth, uncle and nephew, scientist and humanist, are different characters facing similar challenges. Although Benn ends the book once again fleeing from any human engagement, one senses that the younger Kenneth has learned something from both his and his uncle's predicaments.

Resources

The largest single collection of Saul Bellow's manuscripts can be found at the Special Collections Department of Regenstein Library, University of Chicago. A smaller set of manuscripts is found at Boston University and at the Harry Ransom Center for the Humanities, University of Texas at Austin. Other institutions and organizations of interest to students of Saul Bellow include the following:

Boston University. Bellow's academic home is a source of information on his later work, as well as his teaching and editorial activities. Boston University's library also holds some of Bellow's manuscripts. (http://www.bu.edu/uni/Faculty/Bellow.html)

The National Foundation for Jewish Culture. This organization honored Bellow with its Literary Arts Award in 1998. The award was presented by the Romanian writer Norman Manea, who gave a heartfelt and perceptive tribute, touching upon the humanity and humility of Bellow's cultural position. (http://www.jewishculture.org/1998/jcaaBellows.htm)

The Nobel Prize Internet Archive. This collection of materials on Nobelists in literature contains information on Bellow's citation for the award, his acceptance speech, and other aspects of his career. It includes links to many Bellow-related Web sites. (http://www.almaz.com/nobel/literature/1976a.html)

Saul Bellow Society. This group of academics devoted to the study of Bellow was founded in 1982 and is headquartered at Brigham Young University in Utah. It includes members from across the United States and Canada and the world. The society publishes a journal and a newsletter (back articles of which are listed on the site) and sponsors conference panels. (http://english.byu.edu/cronin/saulb)

NICHOLAS BIRNS

Index

Page numbers in **boldface** type indicate article titles. Page numbers in *italic* type indicate illustrations.